SEVEN
MIRACLES
of
MANAGEMENT

ALAN DOWNS

PRENTICE HALL PRESS

Library of Congress Cataloging-in-Publication Data

Downs, Alan.
    The seven miracles of management / Alan Downs.
        p. cm.
    Includes index.
    ISBN 0-7352-0042-4
    1. Industrial management. 2. Industrial management—Moral and
ethical aspects. 3. Success in business. 4. Achievement motivation. I. Title.
HD31.D676 1998
658—dc21
                                            98-23861
                                               CIP

ISBN 0-7352-0042-4

ATTENTION: CORPORATIONS AND SCHOOLS
Prentice Hall books are available at quantity discounts with bulk purchase
for educational, business, or sales promotional use. For information, please
write to: Prentice Hall Special Sales, 240 Frisch Court, Paramus, New
Jersey 07652. Please supply: title of book, ISBN, quantity, how the book
will be used, and date needed.

PRENTICE HALL PRESS
Paramus, NJ 07652

A Simon & Schuster Company

On the World Wide Web at http://www.phdirect.com

Prentice Hall International (UK) Limited, *London*
Prentice Hall of Australia Pty. Limited, *Sydney*
Prentice Hall Canada, Inc., *Toronto*
Prentice Hall Hispanoamericana, S.A., *Mexico*
Prentice Hall of India Private Limited, *New Delhi*
Prentice Hall of Japan, Inc., *Tokyo*
Simon & Schuster Asia Pte. Ltd., *Singapore*
Editora Prentice Hall do Brasil, Ltda., *Rio de Janeiro*

Acknowledgments

No book is written alone. The voices of friends and teachers, present and past, whisper in your ear and tell you what to write. Unfortunately, their names don't appear on the book's spine, so I must try to list them here:

Fredericka MacKenzie, Sylvia Rayfield, and Annette Simmons provided valuable comments to several stages of the manuscript and endured my search for the perfect title.

My dear friends Roland and Jackie Grimm gave relentless support during both the pains and joys of writing the manuscript.

Amy Petty, my sister, was extraordinarily generous in arranging interviews with her fellow survivors of the Oklahoma City Murrah Federal Building bombing.

Ruth Elmer, one of the most profound teachers I have ever known, provided much inspiration and insight to this book through her weekly lectures.

My agent, Julie Castiglia, deserves much of the credit for the publication of this book. At Prentice Hall, my editor Tom Power believed in the book from the very beginning and made it a reality.

Two very special people deserve mention, for without them, I would have never found the courage to write this book: Kevin Sloan and Betty Lynne Theriot.

Thank you.

Contents

Preface

This book took many years to write. It is the culmination of a decade and a half of study, experience and practice. The ideas I describe are not originally mine; they are centuries old and universal in scope.

What took this book so long to come into being, was not the writing or even the research; it was the time it took for me to find the courage to write it. Let me explain.

The miracles described in this book are found inside each of us. I have known the basics of this material since I was a child. And since my childhood, I have been educated in a world that has taught me to qualify, twist, and deny these basic truths. Perhaps you, too, have had such an education.

We have been taught wrongly. We were taught that good business was never to be corrupted by human kindness or compassion. Those were soft spots—vulnerabilities—which would cause us to fail. Hide your human feelings, consider everyone else your competitor, and struggle to get a larger share of limited resources. Work must be hard, and we must work hard at it. If someone doesn't feel pain, there is no gain.

This book is an attempt to undo that education. For if we must be hard-edged at work, we must be hard-edged human beings. And if we must be manipulative, aggressive, exploitative and beguiling at work, then we must also be that kind of person. Otherwise, we are either inauthentic in business or inauthentic at life, neither of which holds much fulfillment. We cannot be one way in business and another in life without living in perpetual deception.

In these pages, I describe what is essentially my own journey back to personal integrity and enchantment. In this search, I find that there have been others, some well-known and successful, who have gone this path before me. They have found their birthright: the power of their own humanity. In their businesses, they employed their full being, attempting to be honest, loving, forgiving, creative and supportive. When they succeeded at this quest, they found a new style of management that transcends the limited, small-minded power struggle that prevails over so many organizations. Their success is what is often called *effortless accomplishment*. By simply being genuine, they released a miraculous power in their organizations that created far more than could have happened if they had followed the usual path of manipulation, push-pull, withholding, power games, and competitive aggression.

I said it took time to find the courage to the write this book. Like most everyone, I wanted to be part of the pack. Do the business thing and make a good living. Play the game and win. I wanted to swim with sharks and enjoy the bounty. I wanted the carrot that was dangled before me by business school and societal myths about success.

But as strong as my appetite for success is, I am also plagued by a gnawing desire to achieve my highest good. To do something that matters to me and to the good of society. To make a difference. To help. To love, learn and be loved. To know, when that last day comes and I look back on my life, that I—the sum total of me—was worthwhile.

The joy of this book, and what gave me the courage to write it, is the finding that material success in business does not have to be inconsistent with personal fulfillment. It is possible to be on the road to your personal best and to build a successful, thriving business. The two are only self-canceling when we are taught it must be so. This is the great lie of business in the twentieth century.

Each of the miracles listed in this book will not only change your organization, it will change you. If you take the material to heart, practice it, and insist that others in your charge practice it, it will change you and your organization. It will take you back to the place you once knew, where authenticity and sincerity surround you, flow from you and toward you. It is the only place where you will find fulfillment as a manager and as a growing human being.

The first section of each chapter is the meat of the material; it is the description of the miracle and how to apply it. The second section is what I am calling "creating the miracle." Here I list a few suggestions for creating the miracle in your organization. Finally, each chapter ends with affirmations for the miracle. These are simple statements which you can easily hold in memory and repeat to yourself throughout your daily routine. They help to focus your thoughts on what you read and to translate those principles into actions on the job.

It is my pleasure to present these miracles to you and remind you that they have always lived within yourself. It is my sincere hope that you hear the calling from within and answer with an affirmative, "I will try." For if you try, it will work. When it works, we will transform the confusion and hardship that reigns over so much of corporate life and lift ourselves to a higher plane.

Alan Downs
Fall 1998

Introduction

Miracles happen everyday.

The extraordinary, the unusual, the exceptional, the spellbinding, the phenomenal happen every day because of ordinary people in ordinary companies. These are not hocus-pocus, mystical, conjured-up events; they are concrete, natural occurrences that defy the impossible and make it reality. These are miracles.

The creation of something extra is the essence of a miracle. It is the transformation of the ordinary into the extraordinary. It is the multiplication of resources, the manifestation of a new reality out of thin air.

Sound impossible? Wishful thinking, but not possible?

Miracles are what business is all about.

From where does the gain that we call "profit" come? How is it that one company can take resources and create profit while another can take the same resources and fail? For example, how is it that one company hooked together a series of rather ordinary circuit boards, called it a "personal computer," and created a multibillion dollar, international market?

Business is about the creation of miracles, and successful businesses work these miracles everyday. They take what exists and transform it into more than what was. Like the personal computer pioneers, they combine existing technology and resources, transforming them into a new technology that creates markets and new wealth.

To put it in more traditional, business school language, an organization is a system that receives inputs and expels *value-added* outputs. Something more ingenious, productive and profitable must be the organization's output or, unless it is protected by a larger entity (e.g., government), it will soon cease to exist.

For much of the last century business philosophers and economists have sought to understand this transformational potency of successful business. What is the elusive formula that allows for the multiplying of assets? How is it that the output is more than the sum of the inputs? Exactly how does something *more* come from something *less*?

We have thrashed about with program after program seeking the answers to these remarkable questions. The list of theories, organizational interventions and management fads is long and varied. Each has touted some aspect of the truth, but none seems to have lasting efficacy. Either because of fickle fashion or frustration, most are discarded after only a few years of use.

Our discontent with these partial solutions has led us down a darkly cynical path. Unable to fully explain and predict the phenomenon of creative growth, we have ignored it. Much like the "black box" behavioral psychologists of the early twentieth century who refused to study thoughts and feelings because they were intangible, we have turned our attention away from what we can't easily explain.

The behaviorists studied simple environmental stimuli and reactive responses. From the responses of rats to electric shocks and food pellets, they attempted to explain the complexities of human behavior. What emerged from this school of thought was an overly simplistic, mechanistic model of behavior that was successful in predicting only the most basic behaviors. Because the behaviorists ignored the intricacies of emotion and thought, they failed to account for the behaviors which are uniquely human.

But like the behaviorists, we have decided that the creative, dynamic aspect of the corporation is a "black box" that eludes rationality, and have opted instead to limit our "interventions" to manipulations of stimulus, response and structure. We have ignored the humanity of the corporation and have deluded ourselves with mechanistic organizational models.

This kind of thinking tells us that the path to success requires the correct manipulation of resources. We constantly rearrange resources. We reorganize, merge, acquire, divest and spin-off. We tell ourselves, "if only I can find the right arrangement of resources, then I will be successful."

CORPORATE HUMANITY

Miracles happen when we honor humanity.

For the most part, corporate manipulations share one common factor: they ignore the *humanity* of the corporation. The humanness of the organization is, without question, the corporate version of the black box. It is the one issue of business that most executives dance around, but are very hesitant to delve into. While the management shelves in bookstores are full of books promoting the humanity of the corporation, senior executives and, more importantly, powerful Wall Street analysts are often headed full steam in the opposite direction.

In March 1997, an article appeared in the *Wall Street Journal* [1] which worried that Pepsi-Cola's CEO was too concerned about humane management. The article quotes one management consultant, Tom Pirko, who complained that CEO Craig Weatherup may be "too nice for Pepsi-Cola's own good . . . what's needed at Pepsi is some basic brutality." Weatherup disagreed stating that he would not sacrifice some of Pepsi's people-oriented management practices to raise the stock from $55 to $60 a share. What was the *Journal*'s response? "That kind of talk hardly thrills Wall Street," it says, noting shareholders would love a price boost, "humanity or no humanity." All this was despite the fact that Pepsi-Cola North America increased sales by 4 percent and operating profit by 14 percent in the previous year.

A company of any size is nothing more than a collection of people and assets. It is the people who bring their energy and power to bear on those assets to create profits and, hence, greater assets. By diminishing the human element, which so many of these popular organizational manipulations do, the corporation is actually diminishing its momentum.

The essence of humanity is contained in two elements: meaning and emotion. Throughout the ages great philosophers, writers, theologians and prophets have described the human condition using these two vital distinctions. Modern psychologists have called it thinking and feeling, or sometimes affect and intelligence. Whatever label is used, the distinction between and importance of these two ideas has persisted through centuries of man's struggle to understand his own existence.

Both meaning and emotion are sources of tremendous power within the individual. Together, they provide the impetus that propels the individual and thus society forward. When one or the other is absent, life itself falls apart and disintegrates into something that is less than human. Meaning and emotion are the cause of all great, creative accomplishments; conversely, deep disturbances of either is the primary cause of suicide.

MEANING

Meaning is thought, and much more. It is thought that resonates with the most basic elements of our being. It is a reason for which to live. It is the cherished knowledge of the reason for one's own existence. Meaning can be preverbal, mostly unconscious, and continually evolving, but its effect on behavior never wavers.

Viktor Frankl, the renowned psychiatrist who survived Nazi imprisonment at Auschwitz, calls meaning and "the will to meaning" the most important motivation in man. He wrote: "Man's main concern is not to gain pleasure or to avoid pain but rather to see a meaning in his life. That is why man is even ready to suffer, on the condition, to be sure, that his suffering has a meaning."[2]

The German philosopher Nietzsche also saw a powerful force in meaning: "He who has a *why* to live for can bear almost any *how*." Given a significant and personally meaningful reason, man is willing to do anything, even give his own life, to protect it.

Emotion

The other crucial element of our humanity is emotion. In his much acclaimed work, *Emotional Intelligence*, Daniel Goleman makes the case that emotion plays at least as great, if not greater, role in human behavior than does intellect. He writes, "passions overwhelm reason time and time again. . . . For better or for worse, our appraisal of every personal encounter and our responses to it are shaped not just by our rational judgments or personal history, but by our emotions."[3]

Intellect without emotion is unbearably deficient, as any book-weary college student will attest. It was the poet George Santayana who said it so lyrically, "The young man who has not wept is a savage, and the old man who will not laugh is a fool."[4]

The grandfather of American psychology William James went a step further, calling feeling the cornerstone of the self: "Individuality is founded in feeling; and the recesses of feeling, the darker, blinder strata of character, are the only places in the world in which we catch real fact in the making, and directly perceive how events happen, and how work is actually done."[5] The very essence of individuality is found in our feelings; emotions are the starting point of our own uniqueness. From our earliest days on this earth, before words become thoughts in our brains, we are driven by feelings.

Emotion, too, has been denied its rightful seat in the boardroom. We, as corporate managers, have long been fond of hiding the role of emotion in business decisions. Instead, we prefer to talk about objective decisions which are "strictly business." Even the word "business" has come to connote a certain no-nonsense, dispassionate activity.

With good reason, we have de-emphasized the role of immediate, reactive emotions like fear and anger which often manifest themselves in such undesirable outcomes as conflict and prejudice. In the process, however, we have also tried to discard more complex and powerful emotions. Feelings of passion, empathy, trust, and even frustration and rage can be of enormous benefit to the company.

Given the central role of both meaning and emotion in human behavior, it is of no small consequence that both have been slandered by modern organizational manipulations. Meaningful work has been rendered virtually meaningless by repeated reorganizations, extravagant executive salaries, and the fact that the self-confirming feedback of one's actions may be completely diluted in the maze of the global corporation. With the loss of job security also came the loss of job commitment. It is difficult to imagine employees who are regularly moved from job to job attaching personal significance to jobs which they are told from the beginning aren't really theirs to keep. Meaning has been drained in large part from the modern corporation.

The loss of meaning at work has left many feeling helpless and completely frustrated. "Does anything I do really make a difference?" seems to be the resounding question. This helplessness, as it always does, has created a culture of victims ripe with blame. "It's the CEO's fault!" "We don't have a corporate strategy!" "Upper management doesn't listen to our suggestions!" The list of hand-wringing, fault-finding accusations is endless.

The working environment we have created is what Frankl calls an "existential vacuum." It is an environment void of personal meaning beyond financial gain. Among other things, Frankl predicts such a vacuum creates fertile ground for power games and self-indulgence.

THE GREAT DIVIDE

In essence, we have asked corporate managers to split off part of themselves, to "check their feelings at the door." How many times have we heard: "I'm not here to win friends," or "don't take this personally, it's just business," or "I don't care how you feel about it, just do it"?

At the June 1997 annual meeting of Sunbeam shareholders, Al "Chainsaw" Dunlap glowed as he presented the results of his first year as CEO. After having fired half of Sunbeam's 12,000 employees and shutdown a sizable number of its plants, Wall Street was loudly applauding his actions with a $2 billion increase in Sunbeam's market value. It was a banner year for Dunlap: he had personally gained well over a $100 million in stock value and published his autobiography *Mean Business* which described in detail his empathy-free style of management depicted appropriately with a photograph of himself in fatigues and slinging a machine gun.

> *If you want a friend, get a dog. I'm hedging my bets—I have two dogs.*

AL "CHAINSAW" DUNLAP, FORMER CEO SUNBEAM CORP.[6]

At that meeting, a reporter asked West Palm Beach business owner and Sunbeam stockholder Richard Rankin about the impact of Dunlap's actions on employees and the community. He replied, "I wouldn't want to be a kinder, gentler person in my own business. Unfortunately, my business would surely collapse if I let my heart drive me too far." Rankin has given voice to the unspoken fear of emotions in business. If our emotions were allowed to surface, we fear they might sweep us away, killing our rationality and business sense.

But for all our efforts to suppress feeling in business, those feelings remain a significant part of our being. When we refuse to acknowledge them, we reduce ourselves and our own humanity. We diminish our potential, and in a cumulative fashion, diminish the potential success of the organization.

All of the great leaders and innovations have been born out of the marriage of heart and intellect. Without the zeal of emotion, we aren't pushed past our own limits. We must feel our work to achieve our best.

When we shunned meaning and emotion, we handicapped our talent; and when we lost our faith in corporate humanity, we lost our faith in ourselves. We denied the power that lies within each person to generate ideas and then work together to bring those ideas into a rational existence. We erroneously told ourselves that success lay in numbers, not within our own passion and intelligence. We have, as Deepak Chopra has eloquently stated, become "prisoners of the known," limiting ourselves to the status quo and killing our own power of creation— our very own power to make miracles happen.

HUMAN-SIZE SUCCESS

But some of today's more successful corporations are quietly following a different path—one that is both humane and serious about profits.[7] Their stories fill the pages of this book.

These companies have discovered that computer systems and the approval of Wall Street analysts aren't sufficient for great success. Neither is a whiz-bang strategy or corporate reengineering. While these are important, one crucial fact is often overlooked: *It is people that make business happen.* Success and failure ultimately happen because of people, not machines, ideas or cost-cutting. Without people, the company will, quite predictably, fail.

People are human, and humans thrive in nurturing environments that include such things as tenderness, compassion and forgiveness. It follows then that the corporation thrives on these as well.

This book is a call back to faith in the power of our own humanity. A call back to our own ability to create new wealth, a truly *corporate* wealth that benefits all who are associated with our organizations. Throughout these pages, we will explore the anatomy of corporate miracles. Most important, we will look at how any manager can create a chain of miracles that can transform the organization.

THE MANAGER AS MIRACLE WORKER

When you strip away all the blinding accouterments of corporate managerial life and examine closely the job of managing other people, it is at its roots quite simple. Managing is nothing more than taking people, materials, and funding, and making the relationship of these disparate items greater than the sum of the parts. In other words, creating something more than what was before. A manager's—every manager's—job is no less than to create a miracle.

The truth is, every manager has the power to bring about lasting change by honoring, not fighting, the irrepressible humanity within the corporation. Every manager, no matter what level or title, can create miracles that change the status quo and accomplish the impossible.

The manager is the salve that eases the pain of climbing the treacherous corporate ladder. The sharp edges of corporate life tear and snag at the most graceful of employees. Climbing the cliffs inherent in a hierarchical organization is more than any one employee can do alone. Without a doubt, everyone who ascends that rugged terrain does so with the help of a supportive manager. The executive suite is a dream that cannot be fulfilled alone.

It is the manager's job to clear the path for committed and talented employees as they reach toward their career goals. He is a helper, a guide and a nurse. He is there to assist employees and to gently guide them down the path he himself has already mastered. It is the manager's job to create an environment that nurtures and motivates.

The fact is, in today's knowledge industries, one hour of brilliance can be worth more than months of work. The manager must help the employees do whatever is necessary to find those moments of brilliance. By creating an environment where employees thrive, the manager hastens and multiplies those moments.

It is only when we employ the full power of our being, both intellect and emotion, reason and passion, that we create unstoppable, lasting change. This is the essence of the miracle-working power you hold in your hands.

The power for miracles lives in each of us. It is as close as our own breath. So close and familiar, it is most often overlooked and remains unused. This power is our one true gift and distinction. It is our humanity.

This is an extraordinary power. If you access it— and it is quite accessible—you can change the direst of circumstances. This power can change lives and relationships. It can change organizations. It can change you.

THE MIRACLES

In the chapters that follow are the seven immutable laws, each of which, when called into service, can produce a corresponding miracle. We can observe the truth in these laws across many centuries of time and across many differing disciplines, philosophies, and religions. The laws are pillar principles of humanity and when acted upon, they dependably create extraordinary results.

The criterion I used for including a miracle in this group of seven is what I call "the unity of truth." Truth, wherever it is found, stands the test of time. Principles of modern psychology gleaned from studies of college sophomores are just as relevant as verses from ancient Hebrew or Chinese manuscripts when each stands the test of time and experience. These kinds of truths transcend the artificial borders which define science, religion and philosophy. Each of the miracles in this book is just such a transcendental truth.

A second, more subjective criterion was also applied to these miracles: they had to "ring of truth." They had to have the immediate recognition of what some might call "common sense" or "everyday truth." Simply, they had to resonate with what we all know to be true about life. And most importantly, there had to be evidence that these miracles were indeed working wonders within today's companies.

SUPERNATURAL POWER

Miracles, by definition, draw upon a greater power—one capable of creating transformation and extraordinary accomplishment. These seven miracles draw upon the greatest power of the universe: love. Nothing else has the power to change the world for the better. The love of freedom and individual dignity has spread democracy throughout the world in recent decades. The love of science and of suffering people has created cures for many illnesses. The love of engineering and design has created new ways of building structures that span great distances and scrape the skies. The love of the universe has put a man on the moon, a robot on Mars and a community of astronauts in continuous orbit of the earth. When the fullness of love manifests, it always transforms reality.

When we fully embrace the power and completeness of love, it empowers us. We no longer focus on competition, but sharing. What more can we give our customers? How can we contribute to the marketplace? What can we do that will improve lives?

The seven miracles in this book are all based on the supernatural power of love. The love of our work. The love of ourselves. The love of employees. The love of the community and the well-being of society. The love of all mankind.

Much of current management theory is rooted in the antithesis of a thought system based on love: a system of fear. Not the genuine fear of real dangers, but free-floating fear that pushes managers to control and hoard power. The ultimate product of this fear is a rigid, unchanging organization that has turned its focus away from creativity and growth, preferring to spend inordinate efforts in destroying the competition, controlling employees, manipulating public opinion and stockpiling wealth. This fearful thinking sees the world as a limited pie where everyone must fight for a bigger piece at the expense of others.

Management based on a system of love sees the world quite differently. Love says that each person will grow and blossom if given the right circumstances and support. It says that trust is always more productive than control. Instead of protection, this system seeks creative growth that isn't limited to today's boundaries. Love knows that the universe is constantly expanding and the key to success lies in participating in that unfolding rather than trying to hoard yesterday's manna.

The seven laws and miracles in this book are true in all aspects of life, but I have chosen to write about them as they relate to the modern organization. In my work as a consultant and writer, I find that no other place is more desperately in need of these miracles than today's organizations. So common, we take these miracles for granted and instead search high and low for something more profound, pulling farther and farther away from the truth that resides within each of us.

These seven miracles have effectively transformed modern organizations. If you exercise them, you will see extraordinary changes in the people you manage. They, in turn, will change your organization for the better.

Peel away the consultants, the hype, the program names and the buzzwords, and what you find at the core of every successful change program is at least one of these miracles operating. What's more, these miracles don't have to cost a dime, but they will demand your effort, patience and commitment. Be warned: as with so many things in life, partial efforts are doomed to certain failure.

Challenge yourself. Suspend your disbelief and feel your own power to make a difference. Place aside the faults of the organization and make a change for the better. You can make miracles happen.

THE MIRACLE
OF
Manifestation

Mind is the master power that molds and makes,
And man is mind.

And ever more he takes the tool of thought,
And shaping what he wills,
Brings forth a thousand joys or a thousand ills.

He thinks in secret and it comes to pass,
Environment is but his looking glass.

JAMES ALLEN [8]

The revelation of Thought takes men out
of servitude into freedom.

RALPH WALDO EMERSON [9]

EVERYTHING MAN CREATES FIRST STARTS WITH AN INTANGIBLE AND DEFINITE IDEA

Nothing new in our reality comes into being without first being born of an *idea*. Ideas are extremely powerful, energetic and unifying. They are the most miraculous gift given to human beings.

The miracle of manifestation is the transformation of ideas into reality. It starts with a clear awareness of the present situation. We then create a mental picture of what we want (the idea). Through the processes of commitment and affirmations, we allow the idea to unfold into our world. The once abstract idea becomes materialized.

Manifestation is truly fascinating and miraculous, and need not seem mysterious or somehow darkly mystical. Manifestation happens to each of us everyday; it's all around us. Our ideas are constantly shaping our lives and environments. How we think about the world creates the world we experience. If you think you will fail at a task and dwell on that idea, chances are very good that you will indeed fail. If, on the other hand, you focus your thoughts on reaching a goal, there is a good possibility you will achieve that goal.

Many different labels have been given to the phenomenon of manifestation. Psychologists have called it the self-fulfilling prophecy and goal-setting. Physicists, like David Bohm and F. David Peat, have called it a universal law. Theologians, drawing upon the Hebrew proverb, "For as he thinketh in his heart, so is he"[10] among many other scriptures, have translated manifestation into the spiritual realm. Manifestation, under all its various disguises and labels, has been discussed in virtually every field of study.

Not surprisingly, we find the miracle of manifestation to be critical to modern business, too. It is central to the value-added function of business. It is, quite simply, the business of business. No matter how low tech or routine the industry, at its core is the transformation of an idea into a manifest reality.

The process of manifestation is at work throughout every successful organization daily. Employees at all levels are busy thinking through problems and imagining the solutions. Once they have the idea, the solution follows. The better the idea, the better the manifest solution. If there is no clear idea, then the solution doesn't manifest.

As profound as manifestation is, we often take it for granted. It happens so naturally for most of us, we fail to think of it as an extraordinary power which is constantly shaping our lives. "Well, of course, we think," we might say.

Ideas flow through our minds continuously from the time we wake until the time we sleep again. Those ideas, whether we intend it or not, create our future.

There is great merit in examining closely this miraculous power we hold and sometimes use carelessly. The art of manifestation is critical, especially in today's business environment where we are in constant need of new solutions to continuously evolving challenges. It can make the difference between sustained success and unavoidable failure.

To begin, consider the organization where there is a breakdown of manifestation. We all know it; it is called the *bureaucratic organization*. In this company, ideas don't flourish and consequently, creative solutions never manifest. Ideas are replaced with rules and procedures. People in this organization act like gears in a giant machine, constantly repeating the same actions. It is a static system that does not respond dynamically to its environment.

In the bureaucratic organization, the focus is not on new ideas, but rather on the perpetuation of old ideas through the use of regulations and rigid hierarchies of power.

The organization keeps churning out the same product, regardless of the market demand. The ideas never change, consequently neither does the output.

But as Tom Peters famously pointed out, the bureaucratic organization is a dying organization. Today's high rate of change has created a demand on organizations that is unprecedented in history. The organization must be capable of generating new solutions to problems which are continuously unfolding. Every level of the organization must be capable of manifesting ever new realities.

Other detractors of manifestation in the organization are stress and fear, the two greatest enemies of good ideas. In working environments of uncertainty and undue pressure, they tend to restrict our thinking, limit our perception of possibilities and result in reactive ideas that are about escape rather than growth. This "fight or flight" response is a natural reaction to danger, and while it may temporarily save our hide, it doesn't make for good strategy. The renowned drama critic George Nathan said it best: "No man can think clearly when his fists are clenched."[11] Instead, the miracle of manifestation requires a safe and nurturing environment for ideas.

Today's successful companies *create* reality. They manifest something which didn't exist before. They start with an idea and then transform that intangible thought into a tangible reality. They manifest their own destiny. Manifestation is, without a doubt, the most thrilling aspect of modern corporate life.

THE PROCESS OF MANIFESTATION

First, let's look at how manifestation works on the individual level. The stages of manifestation are:

1. Visualization;
2. Commitment;
3. Affirmation; and
4. Realization.

Visualization

The process of manifestation starts with a fertile mind where the seeds of ideas can germinate and grow.

The fertile mind is one that is open and uncluttered with stress and fear.

We need to be in a comfortable, relatively safe position to generate the kind of ideas that blossom into innovative solutions. There is a risk of failure involved in any creative act, and that fear of failing, if given enough energy, can block the flow of creative ideas. When the possibility of failure is wrought with fear, we choose to act on old, proven ideas. Instead of changing our reaction to the situation, we react as we always have. Very often, this kind of behavior produces a vicious cycle where we are afraid to think new ideas, and as a result, continue to get the same dissatisfying results. The miracle of manifestation needs a cocoon of safety in order to produce the best reality of which we are capable.

That's why so many experts in the areas of visualization and creative thinking encourage regular intervals of quiet, meditative, focused thought. This is a time when we create a safe place within ourselves where we shut out the intrusions of the outside world and allow ourselves to be silent, comfortable and receptive.

In these meditative moments, we clear our minds of the usual chatter that constantly runs there. As we relax, we focus our thoughts on an image of what we wish to create. It may be a new manufacturing process, a five-year plan, a new office location, a redesigned organization. Whatever the need, we simply picture the need fulfilled and allow our minds to fill in the missing blanks of our vision. As we picture the solution, we often see connections we never saw before, or we envision wholly different solutions from what we have used before.

This process of visualization is used by every successful business leader. Whether consciously or not, these leaders spend time each day clearing the noise and focusing their thoughts on a specific need. For some, it is in the car or during the train ride to work. For others, it is during their morning shower or right before they fall asleep. For each it is a time when they conceive the ideas that create their organizations.

Not every idea that is visualized manifests in reality. Some ideas come and go. Other ideas transform themselves into better ideas. The point is, when the "right" idea occurs, we seize upon it, commit ourselves to it, and thereby transform that idea into reality.

But what is a "right" idea? It is when our imagined solution resonates with everything we have learned.

The right idea is a perfect fit between ourselves and our current environment. It is the idea that functions to fulfill the highest good for ourselves and those around us.

Sounds lofty, doesn't it? Admittedly, the concept of the "right" idea may seem difficult to attain, but it isn't. Who hasn't had the experience of stumbling upon an idea that is so perfect you simply *know* it is right? It is a gut feeling, a knowing, a confidence that the decision you are about to make is the best possible decision given the situation.

Great leaders and thinkers down through the ages have described this experience of deriving the right idea. The imminent psychiatrist, Sigmund Freud, called it the "ah-hah" experience, an insight that bubbles forth from our unconscious and rings of truth. Centuries earlier, Aristotle called it "intuition," an immediate knowledge that is based on universal truths rather than our senses or experience.[12]

Stung by the splendor of sudden thought.

ROBERT BROWNING[13]

Intuition is a powerful force in the miracle of manifestation. Carl Jung once described it as an openness to possibilities and an ability to envision in a single picture the whole. Whatever the label, our ability to creatively imagine a solution is the force that drives every business forward.

While anecdotes of intuitive hunches that dramatically changed businesses abound, some of the most direct evidence comes from research that began in the early 1960s. Douglas Dean and John Mihalasky of the Newark College of Engineering conducted a study of the intuition and profitability of sixty-seven company presidents. Using a rather simple test for intuition, they found that of the 60 percent who had doubled their profits in the past five years, all of them scored above average on the measure of intuition. Dean and Mihalasky then repeated their study on a second group of company presidents and replicated their original findings.

More recently, Weston Agor of the University of Texas conducted a study on more than 2,500 managers at various levels within both private and public organizations. Using a variety of validated tests, he found that "intuition appears to be a skill that is more prevalent as one moves up the management ladder." Further, he found that senior executives tested significantly higher than middle or lower management in their intuitive abilities.[14]

Daniel Isenberg, writing for the *Harvard Business Review*, spent two years studying the thought processes of several dozen senior managers. Each of these managers had ten to thirty years of management experience and worked in a wide variety of industries. What Isenberg discovered was that "Senior managers seldom think in ways that one might simplistically view as 'rational.'" Instead, when the pressure is on and the stakes are high, intuition was the tool most likely to be used for decision making.[15]

All of these studies point to the fundamental truth of manifestation: ideas create reality.

> **When change is needed, we must first start with an idea. Not just any idea, but a strong idea that acts as a funnel for the energy of accomplishment.**

When we need different results, a new market, better products, increased sales—whatever the need—the first and most important step is to generate that right idea. The new reality can manifest only if the idea first exists.

The process of generating the right idea isn't simply thinking about a problem. It is much more. It requires clearing our minds and focusing on an image. Sitting in silence or a deep state of relaxation can help. Closing your eyes or listening to some soothing music may also help clear the mind.

After slowing down what William James called the "stream of consciousness" we then ask ourselves simple questions: What do we want to happen? What does the best outcome look like? How will the future be?

Once we have answered these questions, we hold the answer in the form of a well-defined picture in our minds. We turn the picture, and examine it from all angles. What does it look like? What are its outstanding features? How does it feel?

During this process of "visualization" we must be careful to free ourselves from the constraints of the status quo.

Temporarily, we must disengage from the limits of today and explore what may exist tomorrow without regard to the path that will connect today with tomorrow.

Determining the path of manifestation comes later. First we must decide what to manifest rather than what the process of manifestation will be.

When we try to manifest a new reality based on what is currently possible rather than a clear vision of the future, we almost always go astray. Remember all the talk about the paperless office a few years ago? It never happened, and my bet is, it never will. Why? Because that vision of the future was based on what was *possible*, not what was *needed*. In other words, futurists drunk with the new technology of personal computers made predictions based on the logical extension of that technology rather than envisioning a workable world that is consistent with human nature. The truth is, we like important words to be static. We like to hold important documents in our hands and to keep a physical record of them, rather than just view them on a screen.

The same is true with the book you now hold in your hands. Just a few years ago, publishers were scrambling to purchase the electronic rights of major literary works and setting up divisions of electronic publishing, based upon the prediction that CD-ROMs would replace books. Again, it was a vision based on technology and not basic human needs. Who really wants to read an entire book from a computer screen? Is there anyone who takes her laptop to the pool for a lazy Saturday afternoon of poolside reading? I suspect very few.

The point is this: the best ideas we visualize must be based on a desirable future, not just a cool advance in today's technology or a "wouldn't that be nice" wishful thought. The best, most successful ideas are those which resonate with our humanness and work for the betterment of all those involved. The more clearly we picture the idea in our minds, the more we mold the idea into the best reality for our future.

Commitment

Once we have generated the idea, the next step is commitment. Does this picture of the future merit an investment of your life? Are you willing to commit yourself to making it a reality? Only those ideas which are important enough to deserve our attention and care will ultimately manifest.

Commitment to an idea transforms it from a wish to goal. It becomes more than just a "nice-to-have;" it is an anticipated accomplishment. For example, consider all the freshmen in college who enroll in the premedical program of study. Many enter the program thinking, "Wouldn't it be nice to be a doctor?" After a few years of difficult study and trying to meet the rigorous requirements of medical school entry, the majority discover that they really aren't *that* committed to the idea of becoming a doctor and find another major. So it is with the other aspects of life. If we are to manifest our ideas, we must be fully and completely committed to making them reality.

Manifestation works on a slow clock. In an age where gratification blossoms at the touch of a button or the click of a mouse, manifestation takes its own time and demands patience of those who engage it. Commitment to manifesting an idea includes allowing the process time to work.

We don't bend spoons with our ideas:
We change the world.

Parlor games and other chicanery happen with the instantaneous sleight of hand; works of art take time.

Commitment to changing your world takes time and an extra helping of patience.

When manifestation involves a group, there must be some unity in the group commitment. An idea held by one person which involves the participation of other people must also have their commitment. The greater the unity of commitment, the more likely the idea will manifest.

Commitment to manifesting an idea is not the same as rigidity. Rigid, unchanging thinking is the antithesis of the universe, as Margaret Wheatley has so well documented in her book, *Leadership and the New Science*.[16] Instead, commitment to an idea means evolving with the idea and allowing the natural course of change to occur, inform and improve the idea.

Commitment to manifestation is analogous to a parent's commitment to a child. The child grows, changes and matures. Eventually, the child leaves the parent and becomes a grown person with his or her own values. With manifestation, we start with an embryonic idea that contains all the elements of a more mature idea. As we commit to the thought embryo, we must also commit to the ultimate unfolding and elaboration of the idea over time. With time and experience, we continue to learn new information that can refine our idea. The manifestation of the highest good requires that we integrate our learning and change our ideas.

Affirmations

One tool that is helpful in building and solidifying commitment to an idea is affirmations. Affirmations are positive, confident statements that "speak the idea into existence."

One of the best examples of an affirmation comes from the computer and technology giant Hewlett-Packard (HP). Lew Platt, HP chief executive, said to a *Business Week* reporter that HP "will fundamentally change the way people think about photography."[17]

Photography? HP? At the time he made the statement (July, 1997), HP had never manufactured a camera or any other commonly used photographic equipment. You may expect that statement from a company like Kodak, Canon, Nikon, Fuji Photo Film or some other photography giant, but not a photography neophyte like HP.

But those companies should take heed. Mr. Platt is exercising a well-worn truth around HP; he is positively affirming the company's vision of the future. For example, back in the early eighties, HP had a vision of the future which was radically different from anything that had previously existed in the market, much less at HP. That vision was to take two printing technologies, laser and inkjet, and sell them to every personal computer owner. At the time, dot matrix was the noisy, cumbersome standard while inkjet was still a messy, low-resolution alternative and laser printing was deemed far too expensive for the average computer user. Nevertheless, HP CEO John Young declared that HP would dramatically expand and dominate the market for these printers. Other, established computer printer makers like Okidata and NCR were blind-sided by HP's brazen stance. Today, those companies own minuscule shares of the printer market compared to HP's 50 percent share in inkjet printers and whopping 60 percent share of the laser printer market. Much to HP's credit, 70 percent of all computer systems sold today include an inkjet printer.

Affirmations are look-you-straight-in-the-eye-statements about the future. "We will lead the market with product X." "We will become the preferred provider of service X." "We will place product X in the hands of every engineer." "No college or university will be considered up-to-date unless they own product X."

Affirmations are not just wishful thinking. A company like HP doesn't make a statement to the world about photography unless it is truly serious about following up those statements with actions. This is what an affirmation is all about—making an assertive commitment to an idea about the future. It is a thoughtful step out on a limb. It is a clearly defined verbal picture of tomorrow.

History is full of brave affirmations that changed the course of mankind. Christopher Columbus asserted to the king and queen of Spain, no less, that the Far East could be reached by sailing westward from Spain. Around the same time, Nicolaus Copernicus made the radical assertion that the earth was not stationary, but revolved around the sun. In the early twentieth century, Orville Wright claimed that manned, self-powered flights could be made, contrary to popular belief and accepted engineering data. Just three decades ago, President John F. Kennedy affirmed that man would travel to the moon, an unprecedented feat in the history of man.

What all of these affirmations hold in common is a definitive statement about the future which was based on a well-crafted idea. Each affirmation contradicted the beliefs of the time and radically proposed a future that was a departure from the status quo. It took courage and confidence to make these statements, often in the face of powerful opposition. Yet, each of these affirmations set the future in motion. Putting the idea into positive, definitive statements generated the confidence and energy that transformed the idea into a reality.

Affirmations are an extremely important step in the miracle of manifestation. Once the idea is formed, the affirmation is the first step in manifesting the new reality. It is a continual, assertive statement that attracts the necessary confidence, commitment and energy to convert the idea into a tangible reality. The miracle of manifestation starts with a visualized idea and continues through the process of commitment and affirmations until it becomes reality.

Realization

Realization is the manifestation stage. Once we have generated an idea that is consistent with our being of talents and knowledge, and are doing all the things which are consistent with that idea coming into reality, we soon find that we have the manifestation of our reality.

MANIFESTATION IN THE ORGANIZATION

If reality is ultimately a product of our thought (as we have seen it is), then the organization must also be a product of our thinking. From the very beginning, an organization only lives in minds of those who access the organization. You cannot point to an organization, only the actions of those who belong to the organization. Increasingly in this age of computer networks, multinational enterprise, and strategic partnerships, it is difficult to identify all the various components of an organization. The organization is nothing more than an abstract concept upon which we all agree. At its core, the organization is little more than an idea.

So it follows that the organization is a continual product of manifestation. The idea at the center of the organization produces the reality that may have local, national, or international ramifications. When that idea changes, the reality of the organization also changes.

This is one of the most profound truths any manager can own: lasting change can happen only when the *idea* of the organization changes.

All too often, well-meaning managers have tried to change organizations by altering the manifest organization without changing the way in which employees, managers, customers and shareholders think about the organization. The outcome? The newly reengineered organization experiences many of the same problems and pitfalls as before. The idea at the center of the organization must change if the organization is to change for the better.

So where is this idea and how is it changed? The idea that creates the organization resides in the minds of stakeholders (i.e., managers, employees, customers and shareholders). Each of these constituencies has an idea about what the organization does and why it exists. This is the collective idea that creates the organization.

Ideas do not reside in strategic plans. They don't live on overhead transparencies, vision statements, organization charts, annual reports or training programs. Ideas can only thrive in the human mind. While each of these may be useful tools for influencing the minds of those involved with the organization, they are only effective to the extent they influence thinking. If they do not change the fundamental way in which people think about the organization, *the organization will not change*.

The way in which stakeholders think about an organization is often relatively simple. Consider the example of Mervyn's:

Mervyn's is a fifty-year-old department store chain headquartered in Hayward, California. The original idea of Mervyn's was created by Merv Morris: to provide basic household goods and clothing at a low cost to the burgeoning baby-boom families following World War II. Mervyn's was known for its basic, no-frills, low-price merchandise.

The idea of Mervyn's survived and prospered through the 1970s when Morris sold the growing chain of department stores to retail giant Dayton-Hudson. In the early 1980s, however, things began to change. The American consumer didn't just want basic clothing at a good price, they wanted well-known fashion designs at a reasonable price. They wanted designer labels and were willing to pay more to get them.

The idea of Mervyn's as it existed in the minds of both the company's buyers and customers, however, did not change. The buyers were still stocking the shelves with dowdy dresses and polyester-blend dress shirts, and the customer still associated that type of merchandise with Mervyn's. Slowly, many of these customers moved over to other retailers who were offering more current fashion at a moderate price. Mervyn's overall performance began to slump.

The idea of basic, low-fashion merchandise persisted through the ranks of management and buyers at Mervyn's. Despite year after year of lackluster results and several turnovers of management during the early 1990s, the power of the old Mervyn's idea persisted. Even when some attempts were made to change the merchandise and the "discount department store" interiors, they never quite seemed to work. Walking into a Mervyn's still felt very much like its original idea—an idea which had fallen out of favor with the buying public.

While Mervyn's has had some recent success in changing this idea with their buyers and merchandisers, they have straggled to change that very simple, persistent idea in the minds of their potential customers. They have upgraded their merchandise and displays, but many customers still associate the name of Mervyn's with the old, low-fashion discount department store. Recently, they even changed their name to Mervyn's California hoping to create a new identity.

The idea of Mervyn's was simple and straightforward, and that idea manifested virtually every aspect of the organization's growth. Before the change, new stores were usually located in strip malls alongside grocery

stores and five-and-dimes where the budget-minded consumer went to shop, rather than the local mall where
more expensive retailers were located. The lighting in
the stores was fluorescent and harsh, unlike the soft, flat-
tering light of high-end department stores which was
meant to show off the merchandise. The display fixtures
were basic chrome and the floor was hard linoleum. Even
the corporate headquarters were retained in Hayward, an
aging suburb of San Francisco where the first Mervyn's
operated.

What we can learn from the Mervyn's example is
two-fold: the idea that manifests an organization (even a
very large organizations) is *simple*, and it is doggedly *persistent*. The idea which founded Mervyn's persisted for
decades after it was truly useful. Both the Mervyn's
employees and customers unwittingly kept the idea of the
organization alive and continued to give it power. The
Mervyn's idea was straightforward and clear (which was
one of the reasons it persisted for so long). Despite many
reorganizations and spending millions of dollars on promotional campaigns, Mervyn's didn't begin to change
until the management effectively changed the master
idea of the organization.

The key to both organizational growth and change
resides in the management of the organizational master
idea. When stakeholders think about the organization,
what one or two things come to mind? The collective

impact of this thinking is what forms the energetic core of the organization.

The greater unity there is within the master idea, the more power that idea has to manifest reality. When all employees think of the organization as being the "highest quality provider" or perhaps as having "the best service," the more power that idea has and the greater likelihood it will manifest and persist over time. Master ideas which are simple and unified create organizations which are driven with a strong sense of mission. These are organizations which most often succeed.

CHANGING THE MASTER IDEA

The manager seeking to change an organization (and I use the term organization to mean any distinct and relatively autonomous organizational unit) must first change the organization's master idea.

The first step in changing the master idea is for the manager to assess what the current idea is which manifests the organization. How do most employees describe the organization, its mission and their role in it? How do they feel about this role? Whom do they see as customers and what do they think these customers expect of the organization? The same line of questioning should be used with other groups of stakeholders in the organization.

Next, the manager must take an honest look at the competencies of the organization. Stripping away the illusions of wishful thinking and personalities, what is the organization capable of producing? What talents lie in the organization? Right now, in the clarity of the present, what intellectual and physical assets reside in the organization? What is the environment in which the organization lives?

Once these questions have been answered, the process of visualization can be used to create the new master idea. The manager, with the input of all stakeholders, must formulate the new idea. The new idea must be simple and, while it may change the organization, it must be consistent with the current *being* of the organization. For example, the new idea that HP will become a leader in the digital-photography market represents a big change for that organization (as noted, HP has never been a player in the photography market), yet it is entirely consistent with the current being of HP (its highly sophisticated digital-imaging technologies are well suited for popular photography applications). The new idea represents complementary change.

The next phases of commitment and affirmation require that the manager begin to build joint commitment to the idea and act *as if* the new idea were *already* a reality. She begins to confidently establish all of the processes necessary for the new idea. Most important, the manager begins to speak of the new idea with positive, reinforcing affirmations. She uses every opportunity to speak with both actions and words about the new idea.

In time, the master idea begins to replace the old idea in the minds of the stakeholders. As they hear the manager continually describe the new way, as they see pictures of the new reality, they slowly begin to accept the new idea for themselves.

Once stakeholders own the new idea, a critical mass of unity forms and the idea begins to manifest. This is the final stage of realizing the manifested reality.

The job of the manager during the realization phase is to ensure that the new idea continues in the minds of the shareholders.

Sometimes, especially when there isn't strong unity for a new organizational idea, it can migrate into something that is undesirable. Employees, frustrated with the inevitable ambiguities of change, may color the new idea with negative feelings. Slowly, what was once a very good idea can begin to disintegrate.

If, for example, employees become disenchanted and resentful toward the organization, what happens? A palpably dark and cynical environment manifests. And the greater unity there is in these negative feelings, the more the work environment degrades. Before long, this growing manifestation affects productivity, efficiency and profitability. Inadvertently, these employees have manifested a demoralized organization.

To keep the new idea on track, the manager must continually be about the business of listening to employees and helping them think about the organization in the new ways. When something happens that threatens the new idea, the manager must help employees to interpret this event positively. Maintaining and building unity around the organizational idea is the primary job of the successful manager. The more unity he or she builds, the more the new reality can manifest.

At the center of manifestation is an idea. At the center of the organization is an idea. At the center of each employee's job is an idea.

The effective manager of the organization is a gardener of ideas, creating a fertile and receptive environment for ideas to flourish and mature. If the joy of harvest is to come, the manager must first cultivate the human field of ideas.

For every organization that exists, manifestation exists. The most important question is, what will your organization manifest? As a manager, you hold in your hands the power of this miracle. The choice is yours.

The miracle is yours to perform. What results will you manifest?

CREATING THE MIRACLE

Here are a few suggestions for creating the miracle of manifestation:

◆   *Brainstorming.* This practice is so commonly used, it has almost become a cliché. Nevertheless, it works. Brainstorming is the exercise of bringing a group together to come up with good ideas. The group is encouraged to suggest any idea that comes to mind. It is then written where everyone can see. This idea inspires another idea, and the process continues until the group has created a long list of ideas. During the process, every group member withholds criticism and self-censorship. While brainstorming always generates many ideas, some of which are discarded, it is a very useful tool for generating creative solutions.

One practice I've seen work very well is to periodically dedicate a staff meeting to brainstorming. Each employee is required to bring in a problem to the meeting and the group spends equal time brainstorming possible solutions. As always, everyone in the group must withhold criticism of ideas during the session. The employee then takes the list of ideas and narrows it down to what might be useful by discarding and combining. In the following staff meeting, each employee presents their chosen idea.

Because ideas are the foundation of manifest solutions, brainstorming as a formal process and as a management attitude is extremely important. Every project should begin with a free-thinking, brainstorming stage. The miracle-working manager encourages, even challenges, employees to dream up better solutions than previously existed. Rather than doing it the same old way, the manager supports a time period of divergent thinking where many different types of solutions are considered before one plan of action is chosen.

◆ *Work from home.* In most offices, the phone is constantly ringing, people are stopping by and it is impossible to focus on one problem for a serious length of time. Just when you think you're coming up with the solution—boom—someone sticks their head in your cubicle and you lose the thought.

Allowing employees the occasional freedom to work from home, the library or a secluded office can be a great support of manifestation. Office cubicles, the most common office design today, diminish privacy and hence, control over one's environment.

I have always found it hard to be creative in a doorless cubicle. I felt a bit odd staring into space for extended periods, pacing the floor, or even lying down for minute; yet all of these things I do regularly when I am creating behind closed doors. For me (and I believe for most people), the generation of ideas is closely linked to my physical comfort. If I'm not comfortable, it's difficult to completely focus my thoughts on the issue at hand. Giving employees the time and environment to carefully think through problems will generate better ideas and manifest the best possible solution.

◆   *Resist the urge to micro-manage.* Give each project sufficient time before assessing its progress and outcomes. For example, I was once in charge of changing the company's performance appraisal system. Everyone seemed to agree that it didn't work, but there was no agreed upon solution for fixing the problem. My rather ambitious solution to this problem was to redesign the performance appraisal instrument from the ground up. When I finished, I had designed a technically sound process for assessing employee performance.

Before rolling the program out to the company, my boss had me test the instrument with several focus groups. What an eye-opener that was! Everyone who attended those focus groups found the new instrument clumsy and irritating. As it turns out, what they really wanted were a few changes to the old instrument: a few more scales of measurement and some behavioral examples of each rating. Was I ever glad that I tested the program first. It would have caused quite an uproar if it had been required of every manager.

The point is, if my manager had pushed me for my accomplishments at every stage of the project, I would have been forced to show some "progress." My new performance assessment instrument would have looked like "progress," but in reality, it wasn't progress at all. Instead, by allowing me to generate ideas and test them without the pressure of showing an immediate outcome, I was able to try out the solutions before I was held accountable for my deliverables. In the end, the old performance instrument with some modifications and examples won approval from most of the company, giving myself and my boss a big boost.

Affirmations

I have everything I need to be successful inside myself. I will encounter no problem which I cannot solve. My ideas create the right solution.

I will provide the space and freedom for ideas. I will give my employees the space and freedom to think and create. Together, we will imagine a future which is our highest good.

I will nurture and cultivate what I know is right. In gentle and respectful ways, I will support the best ideas of my employees until they manifest in reality.

THE MIRACLE OF

Reciprocity

THE LAW OF RECIPROCITY
Behavior Elicits Like Behavior

LIKE ATTRACTS LIKE

This is a basic law of human behavior. One response, however intended, tends to elicit a similar response. People of similar interests tend to cluster in clubs, neighborhoods, churches and even careers. We are irresistibly drawn to others like ourselves and to mirror the actions of those around us.

When someone is rude to us, we are more likely to be rude in return and when someone is kind and understanding, we too are more likely to be kind and understanding. Someone smiles, and we smile back. A hearty laugh causes others to laugh. Behavior elicits like behavior in return.

This is the miracle of reciprocity and it operates around us every day. What we do tends to attract people who approve of our actions and who willingly mirror our behavior. For example, when one manager aggressively begins taking over the domain of another manager, what happens? The targeted manager most often fights back with equal aggression. The employee who is unwilling to help others is often left to flounder when he needs help. The incompetent, albeit nice guy, will often have other employees bending over backward to protect him and hide his mistakes.

The miracle of reciprocity operates in organizations every day, yet of all the miracles, it is the one we are most likely to forget. How many times have you heard an autocratic executive complain about the lack of teamwork among her employees? Or sat in a staff meeting where others rush to defend a half-baked idea simply because it was proposed by a likable colleague? Indeed, reciprocity reigns strong in the corporate world. You get back what you give.

> **Reciprocity is truly golden: Do unto others, and they will do the same unto you.**

Our everyday language is filled with the logic of reciprocity: "I'm calling in some favors for this." "You owe me this one." "He got what he deserves." "Lie down with dogs, you get fleas." We have uncountable ways for expressing the barter economics of reciprocity.

There are many examples of reciprocity at work in the corporate world. Consider Columbia/HCA:

In 1987, Rick Scott, a young Dallas attorney, pooled $125,000 in savings with another financier to buy two El Paso, Texas hospitals. Those two hospitals formed the beginning of Columbia Hospital Corporation which quickly amassed more than 90 hospitals. By 1993, the hospital chain had grown into a $20 billion company with 342 hospitals. In 1997, Columbia attempted a merger with Tenet Healthcare, which would have created the largest healthcare company in the United States.

The phenomenal growth of Columbia can be attributed to the art of the deal. Scott, a talented and free-wheeling deal maker, negotiated the purchase of 30 healthcare concerns and approached some 80 more in 1997 alone. No doubt his success lay in Columbia's ability to spot hospitals on the brink of a financial crisis and to arrive on the scene as a "white knight" saving the day. As Martin Brotman, head of California Pacific Medical Center said, "They're very good at smelling blood in the water. . . . They get a whiff and get in there with their buckets of money so fast."[18]

The hallmark of the Columbia deal is iron-fisted aggressiveness. One tactic, as reported by Bloomberg News, includes warning community hospitals that Columbia will build a competing facility nearby if they don't sell out. Other tactics include secret negotiations where the hospital board of directors are asked to approve a deal without knowing the purchase price and terms. More than a few hospital administrators who arranged these secret deals are now employed by Columbia.

Of great concern to many communities is Columbia's unwillingness to continue charity and indigent care services that were offered by hospitals before they were sold. Institutions which were founded and funded on the basis of emergency and indigent care are no longer providing those much needed services.

Columbia has also been aggressive in its advertising. Among other tactics, Columbia rented billboards near the entrance to many of their competitors, advertising the local Columbia hospital. For example, in front of its chief competitor in Oklahoma City, Baptist Hospital, Columbia rented a large billboard across the street from the main entrance advertising the competing Columbia facilities in the area.

What has this behavior earned Columbia? Aggressive opposition. A few of the defense actions being taken against the company include the following: In Cookeville, Tennessee 1,000 residents turned out to encircle their nonprofit hospital and "hug" the institution. The hospital was not sold. In Rhode Island, the legislature imposed a limit on the number of hospitals that for-profit companies could buy after Columbia expressed strong interest in local hospitals. California Attorney General Dan Lundgren blocked a proposed deal between Columbia and San Diego's highly regarded Sharp Hospital, saying it would severely limit the hospital's ability to continue its charitable and trust obligations. Attorneys general in Michigan and Ohio have also raised objections to Columbia deals. In Florida, the University of Miami Medical Center voted down a proposed lease of the hospital after it considered Columbia's reputation.

And these are the least of Columbia's troubles. It seems the aggressiveness of company leadership has spread down through corporate culture and spawned other combative if not questionable practices. Most notably, the FBI recently acquired 51 search warrants to enter Columbia offices and search for evidence of fraudulent Medicare billing. Currently, three executives have been indicted, with the FBI promising more to come.

At the time of this writing, Rick Scott has been forced to resign as CEO. The new head of Columbia, Dr. Paul Frist, has repeatedly stated that the company plans to take a less aggressive stance in the future. In the words of *Time* magazine, "In the end, Scott's hubris may have cost him his empire."[19]

Reciprocity has brought much of Columbia's own tactics back home to roost. The company will be dealing with the drag of its own reputation for many years to come. According to Linda Miller, president of the Volunteer Trustees of Not-For-Profit Hospitals, "Columbia did manage to wear a target on its chest" because of the "aggressive style of Rick Scott." With its own actions, Columbia created an unfavorable reaction.

There are many other examples of reciprocity in the corporate setting, particularly among individual employees and managers. I came face to face with reciprocity not long after I left graduate school and entered the work force. In one of my first jobs, I walked into a management position that supervised a number of organizational development specialists. These jobs required great facilitation and problem-solving skills, as the incumbents often worked at the highest levels of the company, helping executives to solve problems and work together more efficiently.

One of the specialists who reported to me was Peter, an ex-hippie-turned-EST-turned-Esalen-turned-Total-Quality convert. He was a laid-back kind of guy who rarely made it to meetings on time and always seemed disorganized. I have to admit, from the start I didn't much care for Peter.

I remember sitting in meetings hearing him say things like, "I challenged them on their stuff " and "I told them not to drag up old junk." His pop psychology lingo made me cringe. I could only imagine what his "interventions" were: group hugs or something like that. He was always wanting to take teams out on "ropes courses" where they would swing from trees, fall from ladders into each other's arms and then sit Indian style in groups telling each other how much they "trusted" one another.

Sometime shortly after arriving, I decided that Peter had to go. I wanted a well-trained staff that had solid credentials in business and organizational behavior, and Peter didn't fit the bill. As I started the process of relinquishing some of Peter's more visible duties, my first big lesson in reciprocity began. My actions created a rally of support for Peter within the organization. I had executives from the very top of the organization calling me to voice their unwavering support of Peter's work. Some even offered to move him onto their direct staff if I was going to let Peter go.

As I learned more about Peter's contribution to the organization, I discovered that he was indeed very laid-back, unorganized, somewhat undependable and had little knowledge of formal organization development techniques. What he had done, however, was to be a strong support for a number of executives when they needed it most. He had been brutally honest with them when no one else would. He had been behind the scenes coaching them through troubled waters. Using his simple and direct style, he had helped more than a few managers get back on track after facing imminent derailment.

Now these executives were returning the favor and supporting him. Sure, most admitted that Peter wasn't terribly sophisticated or eloquent, but he had been there for each of them when they needed it most. Regardless of his style or productivity, they were willing to defend him against my naïve judgments.

What I learned from that experience has helped me tremendously. Organizational decisions, especially regarding employees, rarely hinge on competency or performance alone. A big component in these career-altering decisions is reciprocity. An employee who has a great record of performance but who has offended everyone along the way rarely succeeds in an organization. When it comes to others, our innate sense of fair play colors our vision.

In my work as a consultant, I have often been asked by an executive to work with a subordinate manager who is in trouble. Generally, these managers have risen through the ranks quickly, showing great promise. Along the way, however, something goes wrong. They becomes unable to maintain previous successes. Others in the organization begin avoiding this manager, preferring not to work with him on critical projects. He or she becomes unable to influence peers and subordinates to get the work done.

All too often these are symptoms of reciprocity. The failing manager is acting in some way that is eliciting a negative response from others. Perhaps the manager has been overly manipulative or dishonest in his dealings. Perhaps he refused to cooperate with others when help was needed.

Helping a manager in this situation requires asking some tough, personal questions: What are you doing that elicits this response? How are you creating these problems in the organization?

Asking questions like these prevents the manager from blaming others for their woes. Very often, this is exactly what the derailed manager is doing—blaming others for the situations he has created. Pushing the manager to own the situation and acknowledge his participation in the problem is the first step toward recovery.

The next step is even more difficult than the first. This requires the manager to demonstrate the kind of behavior he would like to see from others. This means cooperating with the very same colleagues who previously refused to cooperate with him. It means trusting the motives of others so they will return that trust. For many, it can be a difficult lesson in swallowing pride. More than a few have refused to even try, eventually forcing themselves to fail or move to another position.

By behaving how he would like others to behave toward him, the manager calls into effect the law of reciprocity. In time, those around the manager notice the change and begin to change their own responses. As the manager consistently maintains his behavior, the problems with others begin to slowly dissolve. His influence is restored and the career is back on track.

The law of reciprocity is the antithesis of victimization.

It is impossible to be a victim, blaming others for your troubles, when you acknowledge your own hand in creating the problem. The crux of the issue is, What have I done to create this mess?

Certainly, others can contribute to one manager's failing and for that they do bear some responsibility. Blaming them, however, is completely unproductive. The only person who we can—or want to—completely control is ourselves. Since we can't control others, the best we can do in the face of trouble is change our own actions. The wonderful truth about the law of reciprocity is, if we change our response, others, without control or coercion, respond in like manner.

What is the biggest problem facing your career? Your organization? Now ask yourself a tough question: What am I doing to create the problem?

Are others unwilling to cooperate with your initiatives? Ask yourself: How am I unwilling to cooperate with others? Is your boss unwilling to trust you with more responsibilities? Ask yourself: How do I mistrust the directives and advice of my boss? Are your employees slow to contribute ideas that might improve the business? Ask yourself: How am I withholding information from my employees?

The miracle of reciprocity completes the boomerang arc of behavior. The beginning of the circle is a behavior which is then completed by a reactive behavior. When we change the initiating behavior, we also change the returning arc of behavior. Act as you would have others act, and in time, they will reciprocate your lead.

CREATING THE MIRACLE

Here are a few suggestions for creating the miracle of reciprocity:

◆ *Never act aggressively or subversively toward someone else in the organization, even when those actions may go unnoticed and work to your advantage.* I once consulted with the manager of a purchasing department who had, for reasons unknown to me, a long history of conflict with the manager of information systems. At the time, the systems manager was in charge of rewriting the company's financial systems, which included the purchasing department. The purchasing manager, aware that his department was about to drastically change some core processes, withheld this information from the systems manager. When one of his employees brought up at a staff meeting the potential difference between how the system was being written and the new purchasing processes, the purchasing manager dismissed the comment by telling the employee it wasn't his role to supervise the rewriting of the system. Everyone, including myself, got the picture: Let the systems manager fail by his own ignorance.

What happened? The new purchasing system flopped and the system's manager bore the brunt of having written a very costly, useless program. Ironically, the purchasing manager lost his job six months after the incident. Why? An employee of his used the very same trick, allowing him to fail quite badly. By setting the standard with his own adverse behavior, the purchasing manager approved of a practice that eventually caused his own demise.

◆ *Give your employees the benefit of the doubt.* By trusting their actions, supporting their work and not always trying to second guess their decisions, the manager creates the same support in return. When he needs his employees to quickly support his agenda, they return the trust and are willing to help where needed. During times of crisis or extraordinary stress, this kind of employee support can make the difference between success and failure.

◆ *Resist the urge to kick an employee when he or she is down, however dislikable he or she may be.* Treat the employee who falls sick, has an unexpected divorce, or loses a loved one as you would want to be treated during a personal crisis. Where possible, give them room to recover. Your actions will send a clear and loud message to all employees. In turn, when you need their empathy, it will be there.

◆ *Be quick to help others, even when it isn't required.* If there is something you can do which doesn't take away from your responsibilities, do it. If it is a piece of information, some expertise or the loaning of an employee, give it to the manager or employee in need. By doing so, you are creating a reciprocal "savings account" for your time of need.

Affirmations

What I give comes back to me. I will give my best in order to receive the best for me.

How I treat others matters. I will speak words of encouragement. I will offer help when I can. I will work for the success of others.

I refuse to participate in manipulation and retaliation. Instead, I disempower these actions by refusing to return the action. I will break the negative cycle.

My situation is merely a mirror of my own actions. By choosing my behaviors, I will create the best job I have ever had.

THE MIRACLE
OF
Honesty

THE LAW OF HONESTY
Truthfulness Creates Trust

Nothing astonishes men so much as common sense and plain dealing.

RALPH WALDO EMERSON [20]

TRUST IS THE BASIS OF ALL PRODUCTIVE RELATIONSHIPS

When suppliers can trust what they are told by the company as absolute truth, they are willing to do more than they would otherwise. Employees who feel the company is being straight with them respond with honesty and trustworthiness. Customers come to respect a brand name that they know will deliver exactly what is promised. Shareholders hold a stock longer when they know that management is being completely honest in its projections and disclosures, even when profitability is disappointing.

If honesty in the modern corporation is dead, it is buried on Madison Avenue. The "art of selling" has permeated the corporation, often forcing the truth to take a back seat to the dressed up, turbo-charged marketing pitch. These days, no one dares introduce a new program within the organization without seriously considering the "education" of users. They "sell" it to upper management, "test" market it on focus groups, and, if things should go bad, employ damage control; the latter of which can include such questionable activities as discrediting and silencing critics.

The problem with this marketing approach to corporate relationships is not that it necessarily produces blatant lies, but it often distorts the truth beyond recognition. Increasingly, managers promise virtually anything they think the corporate decision makers want to hear if it will advance their careers.

This varnishing and stretching of the truth creates enormous problems for the organization and, eventually, the manager who consistently indulges in the practice.

Taken to extremes, the organization can make major decisions based on programs and products that exist only on overhead transparencies and glossy handouts—little more than unrealistic promises made in the heat of the moment. Good intentions disintegrate under the weight of reality, and in time those unfulfilled expectations come back to indict the manager who set them.

Where does dishonesty in the organization start? It starts with you and me, everyday. Each day we are dishonest in many ways. For example, we arrive at our 7:00 A.M. meeting after a Herculean effort to arrange for early child care to accommodate the unusually early hour. We smile, and act as if the early hour were no problem for us. In the meeting, we support proposals that we really haven't thought through, but because the boss supports them, we throw our hat into the ring too. Poised and intent, we act as if we are really listening to a boring presentation when, in reality, we aren't hearing a word of it. Then, the human resource representative starts talking about the importance of office safety and we nod our head in agreement, all the while thinking about what a complete waste of time this is.

The point is, organizational civility requires us to engage in a certain level of dishonesty. If we were completely honest all of the time, social order would be virtually impossible. So we simply hide or glaze over the truth with something that is more acceptable, allowing the organization to run smoothly.

The trouble starts when the line between these "socially acceptable lies" and the truth becomes blurred. We no longer recognize what is true and what isn't. We become more and more willing to embellish facts, making them more appetizing to our audience. We put a spin on reality that makes it more acceptable to the organization. By slowly building one embellished fact upon another, we arch quite a distance from the actual truth.

Not only does this dishonesty cause the organization to make decisions on "bad data," it erodes trust between members of the organization. Without trust, the essential ingredient of all relationships, the connections that hold the organization together begin to break down.

One of the principles of modern physics which has contributed heavily to current organizational theory states that matter is nothing but relationships. That's the glue of an organization—relationships. Without honesty, there is no trust, and consequently, very weak relationships. Ultimately, this translates into a dramatically weakened organization.

On the other hand, genuine honesty only strengthens the organizational infrastructure. It builds tempered relationships that can bear enormous stress during times of crisis. This honesty is not always easy or pleasant, but it is effective in creating the best possible organization.

DOES HONESTY PAY?

Despite the tremendous power of honesty to create resilient, committed organizations, most of the recent surveys report that the practice of honesty is on the decline. A 1997 survey sponsored by the Ethics Officer Association found that nearly half of the 1,324 workers surveyed had engaged in unethical and/or illegal acts during the previous year. Of the specific behaviors the respondents mentioned, 14 percent reported lying to cover up an incident, 9 percent reported lying to or deceiving customers, and 5 percent reported lying to management regarding a serious matter. Fifty-six percent of the workers reported they felt pressure from management to act unethically or illegally on the job, with mid-level managers feeling the greatest pressure.[21] A similar survey conducted by Louis Harris & Associates for the management consulting firm of Coopers & Lybrand found that a third of middle managers and half of non-management employees agree that "the messenger of bad news takes a real risk in my company."[22]

Dishonesty *toward* the company (as compared to dishonesty on behalf of the company) is estimated to be at $200 billion a year. A staggering figure in its own right, but even more so when compared to the much lower $4.3 billion which the FBI attributes to all violent crimes per year. Speaking of the FBI, the number of agents dedicated to corporate-related, white-collar crime has dramatically increased over the past fifteen years.

How has this happened? Without a doubt, the answer to this question is multifaceted. Nonetheless, one primary factor can be found in the most unlikely of places: *The Harvard Business Review*. In 1990, two Harvard Business School professors, Amar Bhide and Howard Stevenson, published a diatribe against honesty in business, appropriately titled, "Why be honest, if honesty doesn't pay?"[23] In this nine page article, they conclude that there is no economic reason to be honest.

Citing nothing more than casual, anecdotal evidence they say that dishonesty goes relatively unpunished; "power is an effective substitute for trust," deceit is "unquestionably" rewarded, and trust breakers are unhindered by bad reputations. The article goes on to cite story after story of businesspeople who successfully ripped-off, lied to and cheated others. For these two professors from one of America's most revered business schools, honesty is strictly a moral choice that finds little basis in the reality of business:

> **"Honesty is, in fact, primarily a moral choice. Businesspeople do tell themselves that, in the long run, they will do well by doing good. But there is little factual or logical basis for this conviction. Without values, without a basic preference for right over wrong, trust based on such self-delusion would crumble in the face of temptation."**

What Bhide and Stevenson failed to consider is the long-term impact of dishonesty on business relationships. Sure, one might pull off the big con, walk away with millions of dollars and withdraw from the scene to indulge in the spoils. (The savings & loan scandal of the past decade proved this to be so.) But what about the person who continually engages in dishonest practices on a smaller scale? Are we to believe that others, with whom this person must regularly work, ignore the deceit and continue to transact business, status quo? The experience of most working people overwhelmingly says this just isn't so.

Bhide and Stevenson spend an inordinate amount of space in the article discussing such juvenile practices as "sniping" and "retaliation" toward dishonest business colleagues. In their work, they found these practices to be minimal and suggest this means that dishonesty goes unpunished. While it is true that most professionals refuse to waste time on sabotage or retribution, this is by no means evidence that business relationships don't suffer at the hands of dishonesty. Instead, most adults are operating at a higher level of moral functioning and choose to withdraw from such a situation rather than balance the score. When given the opportunity, they choose to do business elsewhere.

The "punishment" for dishonesty more often comes in the form of missed opportunities than retribution. The mistrusted employee is passed over for the big promotion or the offending firm fails to win the contract. Given a choice, people prefer to work with others whom they trust. When it comes to make-or-break projects in the corporation, the trusted manager is the one tapped on the shoulder.

Indeed, this is the case with at least one example listed in the article. Referring to unnamed "prestigious New York department stores," they tell the story of businesses which order merchandise, are slow to pay, and then, often pay only partial invoices after subtracting trumped up penalties. A good friend of mine who owns a design firm ⟨…⟩ nce provided high-end merchandise to two of th⟨…⟩ ⟨c⟩onfirms this practice and tells me that he ⟨… ⟩o business with these retailers spec⟨…⟩ ⟨H⟩e tells me that many purveyor⟨s … p⟩articularly smaller firms, ⟨…⟩ because of similar expe⟨rience … ⟩rthiness seems to have cost thes⟨e …⟩ ⟨m⟩any opportunities.

T⟨he …⟩ such an article being published by one of t⟨he …⟩ management journals and written by two Ivy Lea⟨gue⟩ professors cannot be ignored. These two professors are training the best business minds in America. Clearly, their frequent use of terms like "moralists," "wishful thinking," and "trusting optimists" communicates a certain lack of intelligence or business savvy on the part of the honest businessperson. The real movers and shakers, they seem to be saying between the lines, are those who are unencumbered by honesty.

But they are wrong, and the wisdom of the ages decries their message. Virtually every recorded religion and the majority of philosophers, writers, poets and other scribes of the human condition hold honesty to be one of the greatest gifts of the individual to himself and society. Without it, society fails. Without it, the individual fails. Those who make their way through dishonesty not only bear the burden of possibly being caught, they sever themselves from trusting relationships. They cannot be trusted, and they cannot trust themselves, for they know their own secrets.

In my previous book, *Beyond the Looking Glass*,[24] I document how quickly the self-serving, dishonest manager can fall. They may fly high using the tricks of hidden wires, but when they fall from grace it is often sudden and severe. The much quoted verse of scripture comes to mind: "Those who live by the sword, die by the sword."

Ironically, of the three examples Bhide and Stevenson use to justify their assertion that dishonesty pays, only one, Exxon, is continuing to operate profitably. The other two, Borland International and "prestigious New York department stores" have been hemorrhaging dramatically in the past few years, the former having laid off 30 percent of its workforce and one of the latter filing for bankruptcy protection.

THE POWER OF EXPECTATIONS

As tempting as exaggeration and embellishment may be, the miracle-working manager instead clings to a healthy reverence for the power of expectations. He knows one very important principle:

> **It is always better to set realistic expectations and exceed them than to promise the moon and not deliver it.**

Allegiance to your stated purpose is the core of honesty. If you are rolling out a new program to improve customer service, will it really work? Or is it merely a program of window dressing that will satisfy the demands of upper management and only appear to accomplish what is promised?

SIMPLICITY

Related to honesty is the value of simplicity.

> **The miracle-working manager always keeps it simple.**

The presentation, the objectives, the project, the plan are all kept in comfortable, bite-sized portions. In most situations, humans can handle only three, perhaps four, concepts at once. If the objective is to influence and motivate others (and this is the role of the manager), overloading others with information only detracts from this purpose. The best is always simple, clear and honest.

> *There are three kinds of lies: lies, damned lies and statistics.*
>
> BENJAMIN DISRAELI
> (QUOTED IN MARK TWAIN'S *AUTOBIOGRAPHY*)[25]

One well-known and intuitive CEO once told me that the number of slides used in a presentation was in direct proportion to the "b— s—" being presented. When this corporate leader was barraged with slick slides and carefully scripted presentations, he started digging for the problem. To his way of thinking, only something rotten needs to be so carefully dressed up.

Often, this is indeed the case. While complex flow charts and models are sometimes necessary, it is more often the case that something much simpler will do the job.

The manager who has a reputation for being direct and clear is the one the organization turns to for guidance when it is really needed.

In reality, distilling complex ideas into a simpler form requires far more management skill than an ambush of boxes, arrows and timelines.

The miracle-working manager avoids engaging in the practice of, what I call, "mental sparring." This occurs when a manager feels compelled to offer opinions and criticisms on everything their colleagues do. It isn't genuine feedback; it is one manager trying to establish himself as the intellectual superior of his colleagues.

The honest manager only offers feedback when it is genuine and seems truly relevant to the issue at hand.

Fighting the temptation to be larger-than-life, to hit others over the head with your intelligence and to bewilder your colleagues with your analytical skills is key to earning the kind of respect necessary to lead an organization.

Admitting one doesn't understand something or has made a mistake is also a key element of managerial honesty. Hiding ignorance or mistakes is a manager's personal sinkhole that only grows bigger with time. When the truth is finally uncovered, the damage to a career is severe and far worse than it would have been without a cover up.

> **Openness and honesty about weaknesses almost always enhances a manager's reputation more than it hurts.**

A TOWERING MISTAKE

Perhaps one of the most poignant examples of honesty about mistakes stands in the center of New York City at Lexington Avenue and Fifty-third Street. At that address stands a monumental gem of modern architecture, the silvery-sleek, fifty-nine story Citicorp Center. It is truly a piece of heroic design that appears to hover weightlessly over a plaza at one corner and St. Peter's church on the other. Two men, architect Hugh Stubbins, Jr. and structural engineer William "Bill" LeMessurier, are responsible for the skyscraper's prize-winning design.

In 1978, barely a year after the completion of Citicorp Center, LeMessurier discovered a disturbing anomaly in the structural design of the building. The finding, triggered by a naïve phone call from a New Jersey engineering student inquiring about the design, was that the joints used in the revolutionary chevron braces invented by LeMessurier were constructed incorrectly. While the original design correctly called for welded joints, the engineers supervising the construction had substituted bolted joints which under most circumstances would have been more than sufficient. Now, after the building was already occupied, LeMessurier began testing his troubling hunch that the building's radical design might prove the bolted joints inadequate to withstand powerful, diagonal winds.

Not totally convinced of his calculations, he turned to Alan Davenport, the director of the Boundary Layer Wind Tunnel Laboratory, at the University of Western Ontario, and a world authority on the effect of high winds on buildings. Davenport's research on the building confirmed LeMessurier's growing fear; the building was critically flawed. Davenport described a real world scenario that was even worse than LeMessurier had considered: Storms lashing at the building would likely set up a vibration that would make the joints even more vulnerable. After reviewing Davenport's numbers and the New York City weather records, LeMessurier initially calculated that there was a one in sixteen chance that just such a storm might hit the area. It was a dangerously high probability—what meteorologists call a sixteen-year storm—and it could happen at any time.

One factor LeMessurier had not included in his calculations was the tuned mass damper, a four-hundred-and-ten-ton block of concrete that was suspended near the top of the building and lessened the swaying of the building during high winds. Including that into his calculations, the probability of the structure failing jumped to a fifty-five year storm.

Deeply shaken, LeMessurier retreated to his home in Maine to consider his options. He could remain silent. After all, the probably of such a storm occurring during the rest of his life (he was currently 52 years old) was relatively slight. At this point Davenport was the only other person who knew of the flaw, and he would never reveal the findings on his own. He could commit suicide; a thought brought on as he considered the likely public disgrace and bankruptcy that would surely follow an announcement of the error. Or, he could reveal the problem and try to assist in the reparations. After much thought, he chose the latter.

After returning to his office in Cambridge, Massachusetts on the morning of Monday, July 31st, he tried calling Hugh Stubbins, the architect with whom he had designed the building. Stubbins was in California and unreachable. He then phoned his liability insurance carrier, Northbrook Insurance Company and explained the problem to their attorneys. Tuesday evening, he met

Stubbins' at his home and laid out the gruesome details. Stubbins, visibly troubled by the tragic news about his masterpiece, agreed to work with LeMessurier to resolve the issue in the best way possible. The next morning, they both boarded a plane for New York to deliver the news to Citicorp's chairman at the time, Walter Wriston.

Wriston, much to LeMessurier's and Stubbin's relief, was genuinely proud of the building he had commissioned and offered his full support to fix it. In the months that followed, a complex plan was executed to repair the joints by welding two-inch plates of steel over the existing joints all the while keeping the building occupied. With the help of meteorologists and sophisticated sensory devices, the building and the weather were constantly monitored for any unusual changes while the repairs were made. By October, the repairs were complete and an independent structural inspection found the building to be safe for a seven-hundred-year storm, making it one of the safest structures ever built.

Throughout the summertime repairs, Citicorp had been amazingly silent regarding indemnification of the repair costs. That changed on September 13th, when LeMessurier's firm was notified that Citicorp intended to recover $4.3 million—a figure which was much less than the actual repair costs and included no punitive damages. After consulting with Northbrook Insurance, LeMessurier offered the maximum his policy would pay: $2 million. Remarkably, Citicorp accepted the offer and the matter never went to court.

According to a report in the *New Yorker*, LeMessurier "emerged with his reputation not merely unscathed but enhanced." The article goes on to report that Leslie Robertson, a competitor of LeMessurier, said "I have a lot of admiration for Bill, because he was very forthcoming. While we say that all engineers would behave as he did, I carry in my mind some skepticism about that."[26]

LeMessurier now tells the tale of the summer in 1978 to his classes at Harvard. He tells of his responsibility for the error (even though he didn't directly create it) and the social responsibility of all engineers to look beyond self-interest and consider the consequences to society as a whole. And he tells them the remarkable finale of his story: when he was completely honest about the mistake, in the end, nothing bad happened.

LeMessurier's assertion that "nothing bad happened" may sound a bit trite to our hard-edged, nineties business sense, but when we look a little closer, there is a significant truth to be found here. Honesty is the ultimate form of self-awareness. When we know ourselves thoroughly, including strengths and weaknesses, we eliminate the fear of inadequacy that usually drives dishonesty. Therefore, when we are honest, we create an environment that is perfectly fit for our capabilities.

Whatever happens as a result of our honesty, even if the consequence appears to be negative, it is working for our highest good. For example, what if I continually fail at a task which I was hired to perform? Eventually, I will probably be fired, but, as painful as that may be in the short run, I can hardly call that a "bad" consequence since it appears that my capabilities weren't suited for the job. Another job would fit my true self better. I can excel elsewhere, whereas I was destined to failure in the current situation.

When we lie about our capabilities to ourselves and the world, it creates enormous problems. We must continually hide ourselves and try to be something we are not, and always remember what we *should* be. Not only can we not reach our full potential through dishonesty, we create enormous stress and pain for ourselves along the way. The burden of dishonesty is extraordinarily heavy, sapping our stamina and joy. When we are honest, we ultimately create the path best suited for our true self.

INTEGRITY MATTERS

This is where the word *integrity* comes into play. Integrity comes from the same root word as *integration* and *integer* and is defined as the property of being sound or whole. Integrity means that one's thoughts and feelings are completely integrated with one's actions. It is the quality of being true to one's self. Dishonesty slowly erodes a manager's integrity.

Integrity is fragile, and once shattered, it is slow to be repaired.

A manager without integrity is incapable of generating the trust and commitment so necessary to the success of the organization; instead she must resort to coercion and fear-building tactics. She has no choice but to command others into action.

The manager with integrity, however, can inspire the troops to action. Employees will quickly follow her because they understand and trust her. Because she is comfortable with herself, she is predictable. Once employees get to know her, they can anticipate her reactions. She refuses to make commitments she can't keep and never intentionally misleads or manipulates others.

Errors of competency, as in the LeMessurier example, can be fixed, but errors of integrity cannot. If one makes a legitimate mistake because of the lack of knowledge or skill, it may not be desirable, but it is understandable. If one deliberately hides the truth from others, he is taken for the fool and is very slow to forget the experience.

Conrad Hilton, the founder of Hilton Hotels, was a prime example of integrity in action. From a poor family in New Mexico, he rose to be the leader of one of America's leading hotel chains. Before the stock market crash of 1929, Hilton had purchased eleven small hotels in the state of Texas, ten of which he subsequently lost as the country sank into the depths of economic depression. Known as a man of impeccable honesty, he was able to rebuild his business on little more than the value of his word and a handshake. By 1949, he was able to buy New York City's Waldorf-Astoria Hotel for $3 million, and in 1954 he completed the largest real estate transaction since the Louisiana Purchase by acquiring the Statler hotel chain for $100 million. He writes in his autobiography, *Be My Guest:* "I have never in my whole life found anything to fear from telling the full, direct truth. And that includes instances when 'a little judicious' evasion was recommended."[27]

Integrity, as it was for Conrad Hilton, is a multiplier of leadership. Alone, it isn't sufficient for success, but coupled with business acumen, it can generate far greater results.

People will follow an honest leader into foreign territory where they would allow no other to lead them. This is the miracle of honesty.

CREATING THE MIRACLE

Here are a few suggestions for creating the miracle of honesty:

◆ *Monitor your own behavior.* How many times a day do you tell someone something they want to hear, even when it is contrary to what you really think? How many times a day do you intentionally tell a partial truth? How much time each day do you spend "wordsmithing" your message to hide its true meaning behind a more acceptable sheepskin? When I began answering these questions for myself, the answers were a bit disturbing. I didn't think of myself as a dishonest person, yet I found that each day I was engaging in dishonest behavior. If you'll try this exercise, you too may find a few surprises and opportunities for creating the miracle of honesty in your own management style.

◆ *Keep in mind that no matter how complex the presentation, most people never remember more than three to five points.* Keep your presentations and reports simple and straightforward. Don't attempt to snow your audience with excess information or endless oratory. Instead, condense the information to the "bare bones," giving your audience exactly what they need to remember. Likewise, insist that your staff follow the same guidelines.

One useful rule of thumb is to fit all of your presentation on no more than three pages (slides, or overheads). If more information is needed, attach it as an appendix or exhibit.

What does this have to do with honesty? Honesty is about eliminating the irrelevant distortions in communication, which often mislead others or hide the truth. Keeping your communications simple and clear will earn you the reputation of straight-shooter. Others will soon pay close attention to what you have to say and trust that what you say is true.

◆   *Never oversell an idea, no matter how much you want to sell it.* Sometimes the results of a project are so far into the future, it can be tempting to exaggerate their properties. After all, it may be years before they occur, and who will remember then what you originally promised? Overblown expectations do reflect on your integrity, regardless if they affect your present performance ratings. Over time others will start to discount what you promise and your ability to influence others will slowly diminish.

Affirmations

I will be as honest as I can. I will refuse to bend the truth for my own self-interest.

By walking in honesty, I will create trust in my abilities and leadership. Others will know my authenticity and rely upon it.

My words will be simple and straightforward. I will not hide the truth with many words and theatrics. Instead, I will speak as plainly and as simply as I can.

I have the courage necessary to gently speak truths which might have otherwise gone unspoken. I will not allow partial truths. Instead, I will be honest and completely up front.

THE MIRACLE
OF
Forgiveness

THE LAW OF FORGIVENESS
*Forgiveness Creates
the Space for Learning*

*P*racticing forgiveness, although extraordinarily powerful, is something of a lost art. Forgiveness is the miracle of the learning organization.

Forgiveness is essential to human growth and learning. In our zeal to succeed, we often forget that mistakes are the foundation stones of all truly great accomplishments.

Much like the digital computers of today, when people learn a single concept, they really learn two things: what it is and what it is not. When we learned the concept of light, we simultaneously learned the meaning of the dark (the absence of light). Light has no meaning without darkness. As Elisabeth Kübler-Ross said in her memoir, "I have learned there is no joy without hardship. There is no pleasure without pain. Would we know the comfort of peace without the distress of war? If not for AIDS, would we notice our humanity is in jeopardy? If not for death, would we appreciate life? If not for hate, would we know the ultimate goal is love?"[28]

So it is that failures are necessary to the learning of success. We must explore the terrain of possibilities before we can know what succeeds and what does not; what is profitable and what isn't. When we forbid failure, we also negate the possibility of success.

The truth is, everyone makes mistakes— everyday.

For most of us, mistakes usually aren't devastating failures and we learn from those mistakes so that we won't repeat them. Occasionally, even the most accomplished of professionals makes a royal blunder.

The manager that practices the power of forgiveness knows how to handle the mistakes of employees. To the committed employee, major mistakes carry inherent pain and frustration. Further condemnation and punishment aren't necessary and only breed resentment. The miracle-working manager first helps the employee fix the problem (not cover it up) and then takes a guilt-free approach to learning from the mistake.

The manager who refuses to practice forgiveness, who insists that everyone's "butt is on the line" is only creating unproductive cover-ups. Employees, rather than learn a lesson for which the company has already paid, are forced to throw good money after bad. That is, those employees must invest added energy and time into either covering up the mistake or into converting the mistake into a Phyrric victory—a success which costs more than it is worth. Given the universal law that anything can be successful given enough money and time, the unforgiving manager wastes more corporate resources than he saves by holding his employees' feet to the fire.

RESPONSIBLE FORGIVENESS

Forgiveness is not allowing a floundering employee to *repeatedly* fail. That is irresponsible and inhumane management.

A manager has a responsibility to deal with the employee who is incompetent, uncommitted or unwilling to learn. Those employees are only hurting themselves and the company; they must be given opportunity to improve or be placed elsewhere.

In a speech to the London Business School Alumni, Charles Handy used a wonderful analogy to describe the practical limits of forgiveness. He likens most mistakes to damage above the waterline—mistakes that are troublesome, but not critical. Mistakes below the waterline, however, sink the boat. The key, according to Handy, is to clearly define the waterline for employees. Which mistakes will potentially sink the corporate boat? These cannot be forgiven, for they jeopardize the well-being of the organization. The majority of mistakes, however, are only superficial wounds above the waterline and can be forgiven.

Handy's distinction between forgivable and unforgivable mistakes brings us to an important point about forgiveness:

Forgiveness does not eliminate natural consequences. It merely waives the addition of punitive damages.

Punitive damages—artificial consequences conjured up to punish the perpetrator—have no place in organizational management. While they are imagined to discourage negative behavior, they generate a host of undesirable side effects. Resentment, retaliation and anger are just a few of the likely consequences of punishing an employee. Remember the law of reciprocity: *behavior elicits like behavior*. When we treat employees like naughty children, they react like naughty children.

Instead, we must rely on the natural consequences of mistakes. First, and most important, the manager who has effectively done her job in hiring motivated employees will find that an employee's act of committing a mistake is often consequence enough. Simply knowing that you have missed the mark and failed to live up to personal expectations is the best deterrent to future mistakes. It is that sickening feeling that you have taken a wrong turn, said the wrong the thing or acted inappropriately.

The forgiving manager clearly defines performance expectations. At times, this may include pointing out mistakes which an employee hasn't perceived. This isn't an accusation or blaming, it is gently, but distinctly clarifying the difference between what is acceptable and what isn't. Once the distinction is made, the incident is, for all purposes, forgotten.

Punitive actions go a step further than forgiveness allows. These are steps taken to deliberately diminish, humiliate or create discomfort for the employee. Common punitive actions include: verbally "dressing down" an employee in front of other employees, unnecessarily publicizing a mistake, removing an employee from a prized project, giving an employee an undesirable schedule or vacation, selectively diminishing regular compensation, denying an earned promotion or transfer and a host of other negative possibilities.

Relying on natural consequences—the disappointment of failing, having to spend extra effort to fix the mistake, enduring the public acknowledgment—that can sometimes accompany visible mistakes is sufficient to deter the mistake in the future. If not, then the problem lies not in adding punitive controls, but rather in the employee's commitment to the job and to learning. An employee who is seemingly unaffected by the natural consequences of mistakes shows a distinct lack of passion for the job. In these rare cases, the employee would do better in another position.

To return briefly to Handy's waterline analogy, the unlikely mistakes that jeopardize the organization must carry limiting consequences. While the employee may learn from such mistakes, the cost is too great. Any employee who is *solely* responsible for risking the well-being of the organization is too great a liability. While these cases are extremely rare, they do sometimes occur. Almost always, the best possible consequence is immediate termination of employment. The forgiving manager does not make a spectacle of the firing, but rather acts swiftly and decisively. The remaining employees will get the message without added theatrics and appreciate the compassion exercised in such a tough decision.

David Packard, founder of Hewlett-Packard and one of my favorite corporate heroes, handled a multi-million dollar mistake made by one of his general managers using the miracle of forgiveness. When asked if he was going fire the offending manager, Packard quite simply replied: Why should I? I just paid dearly for him to learn a lesson.

Forgiveness builds a bedrock of employee loyalty and competence. More important, it elicits forgiveness in return.

No organization is perfect. Neither is any manager. If one looks, it isn't hard to find something about even the best company that one doesn't like. Should you be looking for a good excuse not to commit to a job or need a target for your personal frustration, the unforgiving organization makes a great bull's eye. Employees of the forgiving organization, however, forgive the faults of the organization which they can't change.

BLAME

Unforgiveness breeds fault-finding and blame—two terminal illnesses of love.

There is no quicker and sure way to kill the love between an employee and a job than with the battering ram of unforgiveness. It is ultimately destructive and nonproductive.

Much of the current cynicism and low morale in today's corporations finds its roots in unforgiveness. I shudder every time I hear a struggling CEO blame corporate failures on previous management or employees.

While what is said may be true, by placing the blame he is only opening the floodgates of fault-finding that will start a flood even he isn't likely to escape. Blaming a mistake doesn't fix it, and it only creates many more problems.

OWNING INJURY

One key component of the miracle of forgiveness is the ownership of injury. When either the employee or the organization has failed and somehow injured the interests of another, the first step toward forgiveness requires that the party in error own the injury they have caused. In other words, admit the mistake.

> **Owning the injury is critical to eliciting forgiveness, particularly when the organization has intrusively failed employees.**

Very often, all an employee needs to hear is the organization admit that a mistake was made. The new venture and relocation of employees was ill-planned. The reorganization wasn't such a good idea after all. Whatever the flop, ownership allows employees to drop their morale-lowering campaign. It's hard to continually attack someone who has admitted a mistake was made.

Sadly, there seems to be an understanding among some managers that one should never admit failures or show vulnerability. Some have even referred to this as "trading off your power." But nothing could be farther from the truth. Unless there is significant legal liability associated with an admission, it will almost always win more than it loses. Everyone makes mistakes and, should we act as if we don't, it only makes us a target of attack.

The insincere side of owning the blame is the public relations apology. This is an apology that has little to do with a change for the better and everything to do with damage control. It is an attempt to save one's image, not an intent to do better.

In 1987, Frank Lorenzo, the now notoriously deposed CEO of Continental Airlines, took out a full-page ad in *Newsweek* to confess the company's sins. "We grew so fast that we made mistakes. . . Misplaced baggage. Delays. Reservation errors. You were frustrated and angry. And a lot of hard-working people at Continental were pretty embarrassed." Was Lorenzo sincere about the mishaps? Not according to history. Continental's record for on-time service and customer service showed no significant change in the years following that apology. Such an apology is nothing more than an advertising campaign, completely devoid of a commitment to change.[29]

Owning the injury demands that the offender not only give an apology, but sincerely attempt to change.

The quippy pundit of etiquette, Miss Manners, expresses the idea particularly well:

> **"An apology is not an excuse, and it lacks the power to wipe out the misdeed and its consequences. What it is, is a retroactive statement of intent. How well it works, and how soon, depend on its being weighted with a number of other factors about the offense:**
>
> **Is it plausible that there could have been no intention involved or was there a plausible motive?**
>
> **If it was an accident, was it unavoidable or did recklessness contribute?**
>
> **Is it a repeat offense?**
>
> **How much damage was done?**
>
> **Is it possible to make restitution and could the offender do so?"**[30]

An apology that is sincere and followed by a change in behavior can work wonders. For example, in 1985 Coca-Cola Co. reintroduced original Coke as Coke Classic (after a new formulated Coke failed), publicly confessing that it had misread the market. The effect? According to Thomas Garbett, a corporate advertising consultant, "Coke almost achieved a warmth and humanity out of having made a mistake."

Or consider the case of Rachel Hubka, the president of $3.5 million Rachel's Bus Co., a thriving business built on spotless buses, computer confirmation of orders, and well-trained drivers wearing suits and ties. Hubka reports the painful experience of having to refund $3,200 after one of her drivers failed to get a charter of eighth graders to their destination on time. The school called the company to complain about the delay and after talking with the bus driver, the company admitted the mistake and refunded the charter fee. The result? The school remained a customer. The lesson is: the power of owning an injury to elicit forgiveness occurs only when the apology is accompanied by a change for the better.

Forgiveness is a management tool that is at odds with today's "warrior" manager. To some it may seem too soft for the hard world of business, but in the human corporation, it still work miracles.

CREATING THE MIRACLE

Here are a few suggestions for creating the miracle of forgiveness:

◆ *Accept responsiblility for mistakes you have created.* Accepting the responsibility for failures can be difficult, if not career-altering. But as a manager, your integrity rests on it. By admitting mistakes when they occur, you open the door for learning and righting the mistake. Likewise, never allow an employee to deflect responsibility for mistakes. Insist that he own the mistake and learn from it. When the employee learns that you aren't punishing him, but encouraging him (as well as yourself and the rest of the staff) to learn from the errors he makes, he will be more willing to deal constructively with future mistakes. Forgiveness can only be given when a mistake is owned.

◆ *Periodically purge the personnel file of undesirable information.* Find out what must remain in the file and what can be removed. If you keep a file on each employee, make a habit of purging that file every few months and make sure that employees know you do this. Often, employees assume that mistakes they have made in the distant past continue to hurt them and this only leads to frustration. Let them know that mistakes of the past have been forgotten and that you are only concerned about their current performance.

Sometimes performance documentation is necessary, especially if you think you may have to fire the employee. These cases, however, are rare. When you sense it may be happening, hold onto performance documentation a little longer than usual. If a noticeable change for the better has occurred, purge the file and let the employee know that you have done so. The employee will be relieved and grateful to know that past mistakes won't hinder future success.

◆ *Define the "waterline" long before an employee commits a drastic mistake.* Be very clear about which mistakes will result in severe consequences or being fired. If that day comes, you will find your job much easier. While no one will be pleased with the results, both you and the employee will know the unavoidable consequences. Other employees will appreciate your fair treatment of the employee, even when the consequences are painful to everyone.

Affirmations

Today, I will walk in forgiveness. I will forgive the shortcomings of [your organization] and allow myself to see the most wonderful aspects of working here. I will release my cherished grudges against those who have hurt me.

I will forgive my boss and see him as a growing human being.

I will attempt to reconcile myself with a prodigal employee. Instead of punishment, I will choose support and coaching. I will see all employees for who they are in the present and relinquish the debts of the past. I will reach out to help each employee, not to condemn or judge harshly.

THE MIRACLE
OF
Passion

THE LAW OF PASSION
*We Accomplish Our Highest Good
Only When We Love What We Do*

THE SINGLE MOST POWERFUL INGREDIENT OF WORK IS LOVE

Once you know this, once you feel this down to the bottom of your soul, you have learned the most powerful miracle of management. It is so simple, so naïve, so human.

Why do we spend the better part of our waking hours away from family and friends, hearth and home, working? Love. For some, it is for the love of the task. For others, it is for the love of challenge. Some love the prestige of position and power, while others love the altruistic principles of their nonprofit employer. For many, work is a means to provide shelter and sustenance for those they love. Still others work to buy the objects they love.

Good work is love.

Regardless of the object or direction, love is why we work when we work best. When we lose that love, the work becomes meaningless, drained of passion and energy. It becomes uninspired drudgery.

Loveless work is the same ball and chain of all relationships from which the heart has fled.

Commitments from a more passionate time become resentments that seep into all of our endeavors. The joy of co-worker camaraderie becomes stale, even toxic. The synergy of teamwork becomes a scripted exercise designed to hide our personal vulnerabilities at all cost.

Indeed, we are at our best when we are in love. The height of passion is the mountain top from which all great human accomplishments grow. The security of being wrapped in the warm blanket of love frees us to explore our own vulnerabilities, to risk and to create. When we are in love we travel to places where we have never been. We think thoughts we have never before thought. We do things never dared. We dream.

MATCHMAKER

Truly great managers are curators of love—matchmakers between employees and work.

Managers set the stage for "romance" between employees and work. They officiate the marriage and witness the vows. They support the pair, allowing the love to grow and flourish. At times, they are the marriage counselor, helping the struggling employee to rekindle passion and commitment to a job that has temporarily lost its luster.

Much of the magic in management is in matchmaking. Of all the many tasks given a manager, the creation of a dynamic romance between an eager employee and a job is one of the more thrilling. It is part analysis, part hard work, and much intuition. Matchmaking is an art that resides in the eye and heart of the very best managers. Successful matches don't always follow the obvious rules of education and experience. Sometimes, conventional logic is tossed aside and the most unlikely pair of employee and job go on to fame and glory.

Successful matchmakers know the keystone to successful employees: passion. Without passion, even the most competent of employees will flounder.

Zulma Borders was the best teacher I ever had. I'll never forget the humid spring afternoon she did the impossible: she taught a rambunctious ninth-grade class about the soulful essence of literature. It was a lesson I have never forgotten.

The windows which lined the south end of the classroom were all open and the smell of cut grass filled the classroom as the tractor droned on, cutting the grass of the distant running track. It was the kind of sap-rising afternoon that steals the attention of teenagers and fills their minds with wild daydreams and anticipation. This was the day that Mrs. Borders read to us Edgar Allen Poe's "Annabel Lee."

As she started, "It was many and many a year ago. . ." her voice gracefully sailed over the words, dipping and lunging with rhythm and emotion. She carried us away with her love of the story as she seemed to read a poem that we, for a moment, believed was her own. As she haltingly delivered to us the tragic end of Poe's beautiful maiden, it was then I noticed the tears sparkling in her eyes and slipping down her rounded cheeks. Once finished, silence reigned over a mesmerized classroom. She gently closed the book, folded her hands, looked down in silence, and then said to us, "This is what great literature is all about. Never forget it."

And I haven't.

On another occasion, I remember a new student teacher arriving in Mrs. Border's classroom. Mrs. Borders walked in her stately manner to the door and extended her hand. "Welcome" she said to the grinning novice, "to the best job you'll ever have." After introducing the new student teacher to the class, she gave her some of the most profound advice I have ever been blessed to overhear: "If the day ever comes that you walk through that door and don't feel a spark of excitement, that should be your last day as a teacher."

Mrs. Borders had found her soul's calling and she wasn't about to let anyone placed in her care settle for less. When in the presence of a Mrs. Borders, a person so in love with her job, it is electric. To describe such a combination as "work" seems to defile it, much like describing a joyous endeavor as a tiresome burden.

Mining for Passion

Like Mrs. Borders, matchmakers are on the lookout for passion. They look for a sparkle in the eye and a lingering enthusiasm. The elevated pulse and eager conversation are dead giveaways. When the personality and the job effortlessly fit together like two complimentary pieces of a puzzle never before constructed, it is a match that falls into place with a satisfying "click!"

Many of the problems of the modern corporation can be traced back to the decline of the matchmaker. Employees are thrown into jobs for which they have little or no interest. Managers of these employees have forsaken their role as matchmaker and have, instead, taken the yoke of taskmaster. They parcel out work to employees as if they were interchangeable robots; as if the dreams and desires of employees were of no value to the organization.

Dreams and desires of employees are of solid monetary value to the corporation. They are the only energy the corporation has.

Without dreams and desires, there is little reason to push harder. There is no point in improving. Innovation withers.

ENTREPRENEURIAL PASSION

Matchmaking is the essence of the entrepreneurial spirit. The entrepreneur has self-selected his match. He has found a task that is an extension of his own personality. It is a task he creates, nurtures, protects, and embraces. Creating entrepreneurs within the corporation means matching employees with jobs for which there is depth of feeling and commitment.

Sadly, through years of constant reorganizations, little attention has been paid to the ongoing tasks of the matchmaker, creating instead marriages of convenience. These temporary arrangements between employees and jobs are passionless betrothals that are doomed to do little more than maintain the status quo. It is an arrangement that provides the employee with a paycheck and the job with an incumbent. While these arrangements maintain social order and "keep up appearances," they deprive both the employee and the organization of more fulfilling and productive possibilities. In time, employees hardened and embittered by years of loveless work, become dead weight that, with collective force, drag the organization down, slowing its pace and paralyzing its ability to change.

GOLD DIGGERS

Sometimes matchmakers encounter the problem of the gold digger. Gold diggers care little for the content of work; any job will do that pays well enough. They are often suave, sophisticated impostors who pose for any position that advances their bank accounts. Sometimes even the most talented of matchmakers can have difficulty discerning between the craving for wealth and the love of a job. The problem of the gold digger is particularly poignant when times are tough and sacrifices must be made. These are the employees who slip out the back door at the first opportunity, leaving an organization at a time when it desperately needs help. When the gold runs out, so does their commitment.

> **Matchmaking is one of the most important roles of any manager.**

The knack for spotting talent that is magnetized to a job is a skill that is paramount to shaping the high potential organization. Those who would aspire to manage, must also aspire to the role of matchmaker and counselor. The manager who masters matchmaking can compensate for almost any other weakness.

THE CALLING

Above all else, cultivating the miracle of love is the calling of every manager. It is the only path to inspiring the highest level of achievement in employees. While employees may work without passion, they will never excel in its absence. A career of drudgery may produce, but it is always less than what could be, what *should* be. The manager who allows this to happen has cheated both his employer and his fellow man. By not intervening, he allows a worthwhile employee to wander aimlessly without an internal compass and inspiration, and the employer, in turn, is given something less than that for which he paid. This manager costs his employer doubly: the cost of the employee's missed opportunities and the cost of his own paycheck.

Since the corporation is, and always will be, a human entity, it is propelled forward by the unifying energy of humanity: love.

This is the ultimate miracle. Love, passion, tenderness, romance and commitment to a worthy and faithful corporate mission is the key to reaching the highest levels of human and organizational potential. It is the only path to sustainable success.

COMMITMENT

You will never be happy in a job to which you cannot give your heart. Happiness always carries the highest cost; those who refuse to pay go without.

> **The cost of a fulfilling career is no less than the most precious thing you can give—your love.**

Pained souls have tried for centuries to deny this ultimate truth. They have tried to simultaneously protect themselves and reach out for satisfaction, only to find that the two actions are self-canceling. One cannot simultaneously be vulnerable and tough. Eventually we are one or the other, but never both.

> **You cannot simultaneously protect yourself from an organization and give your best to the same. Protection precludes generosity,**

**and generosity of spirit is the very essence
of the creative act.**

Commitment is tenacity. When you need employees to stick with it, tough it out, work the overtime, work smarter and harder, push the envelope, commitment is what you are seeking. A powerful force, commitment is not an instant fix; it is a gradual process that manifests itself over time and trust.

Commitment is a safe place where two parties agree to dwell. In this place, they agree to drop their shields toward one another and become a union. From here they fight shoulder to shoulder against their common enemies, sharing both the battle and the spoils of victory.

Commitment is the basis of the relationship between the employee and an organization. Both have agreed to join forces and work together. Each must let down the shields of protection and share with the other so they may progress toward a common goal.

Commitment is at the core of healthy, productive and fulfilling employment. Without it, there is no relationship.

Tragically, recent times have seen the breakdown of commitment between the corporation and employees.

Both sides have discarded their obligations to one another and are trying to, with one hand, do battle with the competition and, with the other, battle their comrades.

Organizations try to grow and move forward while, at the same time, protecting themselves against employees who would steal their proprietary secrets. Employees, on the other hand, try to advance the fortunes of an organization from which they would steal if given the opportunity. Billions upon billions of corporate dollars are spent each year as corporations and employees try to protect themselves against one another. It is a recipe for wasted energy and mediocre performance.

CREATING COMMITMENT

The manager is the keeper of commitment. It is his job to ensure that corporate commitments toward employees are fulfilled and that employees, in turn, reciprocate that commitment.

Creating commitment requires a vigilant manager. While some corporate commitments are outside of the manager's control, many are not. To start, the manager should clearly define the corporation's commitment to new employees. By carefully delineating the relationship at its outset, new employees set appropriate expectation levels, helping to prevent future disappointments and perceived breaches of commitment.

The manager creating the miracle of commitment keeps a well-tuned eye toward employee loyalty. At the first sign of waning, the manager must intervene. What has happened to breach the relationship? Can trust and commitment be restored?

A grave mistake for any management team is to blatantly disregard the committed relationship between employees and the organization. Sometimes, when there is a changing of the guard in senior managers, new managers do just this. They trample on employee trust as they dismantle the commitments they inherited from previous managers. What they find, however, is that change for the better is not possible until they reestablish the trust they too quickly discarded. Organizational commitments are important to employees, regardless of which decision makers originated them. Broken commitments create a psychological debt that must be satisfied before new commitments can be made.

FIDELITY

The miracle of passion not only demands commitment, it requires fidelity as well. Implicit in the passion between employee and organization is that both will be faithful to each other.

Organizational fidelity is of far more importance than many managers realize. Too often, once an employee is hired, no matter how qualified, that employee becomes something less than someone of equivalent qualifications on the outside. This corporate roving eye is enticed by what it doesn't have and bored with what it does. When exciting new projects come up, outside consultants and employees of competitors become irresistible while those of equal merit on the payroll are ignored. When the organization reaches outside of itself, ignoring those inside who are committed and competent, passion begins to die.

The same is true when new employees are hired at significantly higher salaries than those already employed. It is something of a slap in the face when employees realize that the only way to increase their paycheck is to break their commitment to the organization and court other employers.

WORKING THE STREET

Fidelity is a two-way street. Employees cannot give their best to the organization and, at the same time, shop for a new job.

An employee with "paper on the street" must instinctively pull back from the organization with which his future is unclear. Despite the advice of many career counselors, the continual romancing of headhunters and other employers introduces a critical breach in the employment relationship. If it continues for any period of time, that breech becomes a serious liability to the organization as a less than committed employee continues to draw the same paycheck and give less in return.

Once again, the role of the manager is critical in maintaining fidelity. He has an obligation to his employees to market the skills of his competent and committed subordinates to upper management as opportunities become available. Further, he should always consider current employees before going outside the organization for a new hire. He is obligated to encourage employees whom he discovers are exploring other employment to either move on or recommit themselves to the organization.

Commitment and fidelity are serious components of passion. When broken, they cause the organization to bleed in ways that are not readily apparent, but imminently dangerous.

The manager as caretaker of the corporation must watch for signs of broken commitment and act quickly to restore the relationship between employees and the organization. Without the healing touch of management, broken commitments will never heal. They only grow and fester, draining the organization of much needed energy and, yes, love.

CREATING THE MIRACLE

Here are a few suggestions for creating the miracle of passion:

◆ *Make it a point to discover what each employee loves about his or her job.* Make a list with each employee in one column and what each employee is passionate about in his work in a second column. Can you list this for each employee? Are there some employees for which you can't list a passion that relates to their job? If there isn't anything they love, ask yourself "How should this job be changed?" Or, "Is there some other place where the employee might be more passionate?" You can't afford not to have each employee passionate about their work, otherwise they are giving less than what could be given.

◆ *Examine what you truly love about your job.* Make a list. Now, in a second column, list all the things you don't love about your job. Which column contains the most important items to you?

◆   *In a group meeting, ask employees to list all of the commitments they feel have been made between the company and themselves.* Which ones have been broken? Which ones have been "rewritten" so many times they are meaningless? Now, ask the employees how they think commitments can be kept on both sides. Which commitments should never be broken?

Affirmations

Today, I will focus on what I love about my job. I will spend time doing the tasks I enjoy. Transcending my frustrations, I will rekindle the passion for my work.

My employees are gifts. I will help them to give the most to themselves and to the organization.

Love is my power. I will seek to use my power to it fullest potential.

THE MIRACLE
OF
Esteem

THE LAW OF ESTEEM
*Esteem is Essential
to Productive Relationships*

THE SUCCESSFUL MANAGER HOLDS EACH OF HIS EMPLOYEES IN HIGH ESTEEM

They are her crowning achievement. The manager believes in them, expects much of them and always holds their best interest as a priority. By doing so, she gives them the gifts of pride and confidence which, in turn, empower them to accomplish more than they thought possible and more than she expected. This is the miracle of esteem.

High esteem is not mimicry; it is not narcissistic mirroring, nor is it hiring carbon copies of oneself. It is, quite simply, admiration of individuality.

Esteem is respect and trust in an employee's judgment and ability to perform a job well. It is knowing that an employee will do a job differently than you, but in the end, he will produce the result you both desire. The basis of esteem is understanding and agreement on results.

The successful manager gives employees the freedom to explore and learn new methods of work.

While she gently steers employees from known pitfalls, she never limits them to her own view of how their job should be done. The manager knows that an employee can achieve his best only by accessing his inner ability—his own way of doing the job. If employees work identically, they fail identically. When they work individually, they complement each other's weaknesses and produce something better than any could have produced alone.

Esteem is an essential element between the successful manager and employee. It is the foundation on which a productive and trusting relationship develops.

Where there is no esteem, there is doubt and fear.

Sadly, there are many managers who have not discovered the miracle of esteem. Instead, they treat their employees as if they were incompetent and unworthy of respect. These managers often rely on fear and threats, trying to push their employees further. They speak disparagingly about their employees behind their backs and are disingenuous when face to face. These tactics only decrease the confidence and creativity of employees.

FEUDAL MANAGEMENT

Marjorie Kelly, editor of *Business Ethics*, noted in that magazine's tenth anniversary issue that a distinct division of status exists in many corporations. She writes:

> **"It's based on an archaic notion: that property owners (i.e., shareholders) are a higher class of being whose interests are paramount, while workers are a lower class who exist only to serve. This makes it permissible, even mandatory, to reduce wages paid to one group, so as to increase profits paid to another. . .It's a premise that says stockholders are citizens of the corporation, while employees are subjects.**
>
> **It's uncannily similar to the feudal structure, which said the aristocracy was society, and everyone else existed to serve them. It's similar to the imperial structure that said India existed to enrich Great Britain. Or to the plantation structure that said slaves existed to enrich their masters.[31]"**

What Kelly describes is a management system that lacks esteem for those who do the actual work. In this system, managers and shareholders see themselves as more important than the workers they employ.

Recently, I was dining with a good friend who has attained great success as a money manager. Throughout his career, which has spanned over five decades, he has sat on the boards of directors of many *Fortune 500* companies and on the board of regents of two Ivy League universities. While casually discussing the growing pay gap within many corporations, he voiced the unspoken attitude of so many: "Don't you think that many employees are where they are because they aren't competent or bright enough to be promoted or to make enough money to buy stock?" He felt confident that those at the bottom of the corporate food chain were there because of some personal deficiency. He gave voice to the unspoken belief that is held in some chief executive offices.

This lack of esteem, this smugness of management and shareholders, costs many organizations dearly. It only magnifies the feelings of "have and have-nots." It creates a caste system within the organization that leads to conflict and inefficiency. It is completely unnecessary and destructive.

The hallmarks of organizational aristocracy are rampant in some organizations.

The size of a manager's office reflects his position within the power structure. The quality of furniture, whether the office has windows or carpet, a company car, a secretary, all of these things are doled out to signify one's *status* rather than need. They exist as permanent reminders that this person is more important than those who do not have such amenities.

I have worked with many organizations where near entry-level employees were doing some of the most important work in the organization. Often, these are the ones are dealing directly with customers, suppliers, and the general public. Their actions and attitudes represent the organization to the outside.

A retail store can buy the finest assortment of merchandise, but if the sales clerk isn't helpful or doesn't display the merchandise properly, sales decline. High-tech companies often depend upon their new-hire engineers for the latest advance in technology that will keep the company competitive. No amount of high-level analysis, decision making, conference calls or executive retreats will solve this kind of problem. In this chain of events, the "lowest-level" employee is the critical link.

Instead of handing out status symbols, the organization that truly values its work distributes these amenities on an as-needed basis. The hot-shot engineer that holds many patents may need a secretary more than the vice president three levels above him. The human resource representative who deals with highly confidential issues on a daily basis may need the walled office more than her manager who is mostly involved in project management. Rather than promoting status, these organizations are supporting those who are doing the work—that brings in the revenue—creates the profit, and pays the dividend and management salaries.

NO MORE "KITA"

In 1968, Frederick Herzberg published an article titled "One more time: How do you motivate employees?" in the *Harvard Business Review*.[32] In the thirty years since then, that article continues to sell in reprint form, having sold well over a million copies. Herzberg made a simple, but elegant point in this article which is as relevant today as it was back then. Management actions which function as a "kick in the ass," or KITA, are not effective motivators. Why? They are demeaning, produce resentment, and eventually diminish an employee's performance.

Herzberg made the observation that KITA, despite the negative consequences, is very popular with American managers. In an update to the article published in 1987, he notes that "we seem to be losing ground to KITA." A tyrannical bottom-line mentality that values shareholder dividends and management salaries over the welfare of workers is causing a steady rise in KITA practices. Produce the numbers, or you're out of here. Make your goal, and you get the corner office.

There is a fundamental difference between the manager who uses KITA and the one who chooses the path of esteem. The KITA manager is an essential pedagogue—a demanding schoolmaster—who insists that employees make the grade and pass the test. He looks down upon the employee and is constantly assessing her progress. When the employee falls short, punishments are meted out, and when she succeeds, prizes are awarded.

The manager who practices esteem treats the employee as an equal and supports him in his quest for accomplishment. There is no need for the employee to "prove" himself, he is already a valued member of the team. Instead, the manager functions as an assistant, or a coach when one is needed. Her attitude from the very beginning communicates trust and respect in the employee's ability to do the job. The employee is not struggling to make the grade, but to be his very best. The esteem of his manager supports him in this quest.

In 1968 a landmark book in the field of education was published titled *Pygmalion in the Classroom*. The title refers back to George Bernard Shaw's play, *Pygmalion* where a cockney flower girl is transformed into a fine lady simply because her speech coach believes in her. The book chronicles a classroom of students where the teacher was told (falsely) that some of her students were reaching an "inflection point" in their intellectual development and could be expected to make great scholastic strides over the next year. The teacher was told exactly which students would be the "bloomers." At the beginning and end of the school year, all students were given an IQ test. The result? Although the students who had been labeled "bloomers" were, in reality, randomly selected, they all showed significant gains in IQ points at the end of year. The gain was attributed solely to the teacher's higher expectations of the "bloomer" students.

The *Pygmalion* study stirred an uproar among academics, and by 1982, more than a hundred similar studies had been published, each more or less confirming the findings. The expectations of the teacher had actually contributed to the success of the students.

So it is in the organization. The expectations of a manager can have significant impact on the performance of employees. In ways of which he isn't always conscious, the manager supports and encourages the performance of those he respects and expects to do well. Likewise, those for whom he holds little esteem are adversely affected.

WHERE IT STARTS

To list all of the management behaviors that illustrate esteem would be impossible. That's because esteem isn't a behavior or set of behaviors, it is an *attitude*. Esteem originates out of a place of faith—an abiding belief in those who work for you. All the empowerment programs and all of their excellent activities won't work unless you start with faith in your employees. That is esteem.

Once you trust the competency of your employees, you can let go of the unnecessary control which is based in fear.

In order to succeed, you no longer need to make all the decisions. You trust in your employees' abilities to the best possible job given the resources. Once you've provided those, you step back and watch it happen. The manager who knows the miracle of esteem acts more as an assistant to employees than a taskmaster, surrogate parent, or any of the other failed models of traditional management.

WHOLE FOODS

One of the many wonderful things about living in Austin, New Orleans, San Francisco, or any of two dozen other places in America is a smallish supermarket named Whole Foods. In New Orleans, if you saunter from the French Quarter down Esplanade Avenue, you're bound to run into this delightful market. Tucked between a bohemian-style coffee shop and a Dairy-Queen-turned-award-winning restaurant, is the Whole Foods market. Inside you'll find gleaming produce stacked high and perfectly arranged, mouth-watering baked goods, one of the finest collections of affordable wine, cruelty-free cosmetics and hygiene supplies, every herb and spice known to man, and best of all—the smell of fresh baked bread will follow you throughout the store. Everyone from checkers to produce stockers are knowledgeable and eager to help.

Whole Foods is one of the world's biggest experiments in democratic capitalism. And it is working marvelously. The company is now the largest natural-foods grocer in the United States. As of this writing, it has 43 stores in ten states, revenues of $500 million and net profits which are double the industry average. By the year 2000 the company plans to expand to 100 stores and a billion dollars in revenue.

The organizational culture at Whole Foods is based on respect and esteem for all workers. The company doesn't just mouth the lingo of empowerment, it takes those values very seriously. To start with, executive salaries are limited to eight times the average wage paid to workers. All salaries, including bonuses, are published and available to every worker, at every store. In fact, the company shares so much information about the business with employees, everything from salaries to store sales and profit margins, that the SEC classifies all 6,500 employees as "insiders" for stock-trading purposes.

Cofounder and CEO, John Mackey, explains the culture this way: "Whole Foods is a social system. It's not a hierarchy. We don't have lots of rules handed down from headquarters in Austin. We have lots of self-examination going on."

The company communicates its esteem for workers by allowing them through their teams to have a say in almost every decision that affects them or their store. For example, when new employees are hired, everyone on a team gets to vote, and it takes a two-thirds majority before the candidate is hired. Then, there is a thirty-day trial period at the end of which the team can vote to make the employee full time or, if it isn't working out, let the new employee go.

The team has good reason to carefully examine their performance: bonuses. Whole Foods' "gainsharing" program is tied directly to team performance using sales-per-labor-hour as the metric. Consequently, a nonperforming new employee hurts everyone on the team.

Ultimately, teams and their team leaders make decisions about how they will run their business. They decide such crucial factors as labor spending, ordering and even pricing. Whole Food's management trusts each team to do the best thing for their customers and for the business.

The end result of the team concept is that managers don't worry about making employees work or follow the rules. Everyone on the team is personally responsible for their own performance. Ron Megahan, a store manager, says "I'm not the one you need to impress. It's your fellow team members. And they will be as tough as they can be, because ultimately (the hiring decision) will be a reflection on them."

That's not to say that the teams aren't accountable to management, because they are in a big way. One of the main vehicles for accountability, besides bottom-line financial results, is the Store Tour. On a scheduled basis, each store is toured by a group of employees from another region in the company. The tour lasts for two days and is exhaustive, examining everything from merchandise, displays, and store cleanliness, to team performance.

In addition to the Store Tour, ten times a year each store is paid a surprise visit by a headquarters executive who rates the store on 300 different items. Once a month, every store's TCS results are published companywide, creating a great desire within the company to be the best store.

Whole Foods employees are trusted to handle sensitive information and to make critical business decisions. Corporate management, rather than handing down decisions or restrictive policies, concerns itself with giving each store what it needs to be successful. It is fundamentally a different approach than traditional management; it is one that is steeped in trust and esteem for all employees.

Breach of Trust

So what happens when an employee violates that trust? Consider this first-hand account originally published in *Inc.* magazine from Michael Powell, CEO of Powell's Bookstores, based in Portland, Oregon:[33]

"At Powell's Bookstores, empowerment and decision sharing are not just buzzwords. We work hard to give our employees responsibility and authority throughout the company. We practice that philosophy because it's good business and because we want to be a business that operates on trust and respect. Unfortunately, I had to reexamine those principles last year, after discovering that an employee had stolen more than $60,000 from the company. As a result, we changed some of our security systems. Yet in terms of what's important, we didn't change a thing.

Since I started my company, 25 years ago, I have sought to create an environment in which employees have authority, are trusted, and, yes, are empowered to act on their own. Most large bookstores, for example, have one buyer who makes all the inventory decisions; at

Powell's, about 70 percent of the employees have a voice. We share our profit-and-loss statements with employees, and we have roughly 30 or 40 working committees reviewing every aspect of our operations, from implementing a policy of national advertising to integrating the purchase of inventory as the company has grown to seven stores. Everyone is expected to answer the phones, respond to electronic requests, and deal with customer problems. We want the people working with customers to have the authority to make decisions.

That culture of trust was seriously challenged when an employee was caught with his hand in the till. While copying some paper work one afternoon last spring, a staffer discovered a suspicious pattern in the authorization of cash payouts for used books. All the slips were authorized by one person. The staffer alerted a manager, who investigated the matter and found that this same person had in fact approved a significant number of large cash authorizations. Now, that was possible because employees are encouraged to do multiple tasks during the day. Someone could write a large cash authorization and then work at a cash register, and in effect pay himself. When confronted with that pattern, our employee confessed. In fact, he discussed fairly freely how he had bilked the company. Over the past two years not only had he been stealing cash, but he had been using his responsibility of closing the store as an opportunity to steal books as well. We contacted the police, who turned the matter over to the district attorney, who chose to prosecute.

Now, my first reaction was a kind of numbness and denial. I reacted by looking for any explanation that this wasn't what it appeared to be. But the evidence of theft was overwhelming. And, oddly, once I acknowledged what had happened, I felt angry with myself—angry for having such vulnerable systems. I had a momentary impulse to go out and lock everything up—to start treating everybody as a potential thief. A word of caution, folks. If you think that a thief is a certain type and that you can somehow identify that type by appearance and behavior, you're wrong. In a thousand years, I wouldn't have picked this person. He was earnest, he seemed dedicated, and he was stealing from us.

It was painful to realize that we were operating so naïvely. Our systems were based more on trust than on responsibility. So we made some immediate changes. Our bookkeeping department put some safeguards into place to stop the kinds of opportunities this person had exploited. We stopped the practice of having one person close the stores. And we formed a security committee to change methods of managing cash and to improve systems company wide.

The incident was a watershed for me and my staff, dispelling any naïveté we may have had about crime. We realized that not only can theft happen; it will happen. At the same time, dealing with the matter forced us to revisit our basic values and managerial philosophies. We believe that the modern demands of business call for an empowered and fully flexible staff, and we know that such a staff will often have to handle valuable commodities and money. We also believe that most people are not going to abuse our trust if they are put in a position with a reasonable amount of review and responsibility.

So we had to resist the temptation to just suddenly go out and slap controls over things. That's not the answer. The way to deal with theft is to hire the right people and to put into place the best systems for handling money. And to talk a lot in the company about what it means when someone steals.

Do I believe that sooner or later someone else will steal from us? Absolutely. Do I believe, in the meantime, that having 300 people making independent decisions on the floor is more valuable than being preoccupied about theft to the point of reducing my employees' ability to make decisions? Absolutely. There is a cost-benefit curve here: You have to minimize the cost of theft and maximize the opportunity of having an empowered workforce. So today we have zero tolerance for theft. If people are caught, they are punished fully. But on the other hand, we don't make people go through a metal detector or strip-search them as they go through the door. We are still prepared to tip the scales on the side of the belief that if employees are treated in a respectful and responsible manner, they will be respectful and responsible themselves.

As I sat in the courtroom and watched my former employee being marched off to jail, I felt no triumph or vindication. I wanted to be angry with him, but what I really felt was sadness—even an odd twinge of complicity. I didn't know why this person chose to abuse our company and the trust it puts in its employees. He didn't seem to be angry with us, nor did he have a gambling or drug addiction. Any of those explanations would, in a perverse sort of way, have helped explain things better. But he was stealing simply because he could. Because the money and the books were there. And so I felt sad at realizing that the motivations of people are so complex that a manager or an owner could never begin to understand the permutations of them all. You can't be responsible for what people bring to you. You can be responsible only for the place they come to."

> **Esteem is the fuel that allows employees to soar, knowing that they have all the support they need.**

It is the boost of confidence that lifts him from "good enough" to the best that is possible. Esteem enables and empowers his highest potential.

CREATING THE MIRACLE

Here are a few suggestions for creating the miracle of esteem:

◆ *Take a hard look at your management style.* How often do you direct employees to do a task simply because it is the way you would do it? It's so easy for a manager to fall into the habit of imposing his "style" onto employees, particularly when the pressure for success is high. You can work the miracle of esteem by respecting employees' own style of performing a task. As long as they are safe and getting results, why not allow them the freedom to work in their way? This is esteem in action.

For example, I once knew a manager that reviewed every memo, letter or report that was written by his staff. Inevitably, he would make some correction in the wording or the content to make it more like his own style of communication. Despite the fact that he wasn't a particularly talented letter writer, he always felt the need to impose his ideas on the written communications of his staff. The staff, on the other hand, resented this greatly. He would have earned much more respect had he trusted them to communicate in their own voice.

◆ *Never, never speak ill of an employee, no matter how frustrated or angry you may be.* Although there are times when it just feels good to lambaste a particularly frustrating employee behind his back, you will do well to resist the temptation. Words spoken in angry confidence almost always find their way back to the person about which they are spoken. Those words will continue to speak volumes of disrespect not only to that employee, but everyone else who heard them.

Likewise, never allow an employee to berate or make fun of another employee in your presence. The very fact that you are present when such things are said implies your approval. By discouraging such comments, you win the respect of all employees who will appreciate your fairness.

Affirmations

I hold respect and honor for each of my employees. Each has a unique gift to give. I will see the best in everyone.

Punishment has no place for me. I will coach and carefully direct employees who fail.

My business relationships are the most important part of my business. I will respect and nurture each relationship.

THE MIRACLE
OF
Transcending the Past

THE LAW OF
TRANSCENDING THE PAST
*The Past Has Only the Power
It Is Given*

Never let yesterday use up too much of today.

WILL ROGERS [34]

MEMORY IS THE ESSENTIAL SELF

It is our identity. It is who we know ourselves to be. Without memory, self ceases to exist and life makes little sense.

The *remembered* past defines us in the present and largely determines our future. It is the source of individualism. It is extremely powerful in its effect on our lives. When managers access the power of memory, miracles are created.

Several years ago, I lived in New Orleans, Louisiana. Situated near the mouth of the mighty Mississippi river, New Orleans was carved out of swamp land alongside a crescent bend in the river. Much of the city lies under sea level and remains dry only because of a complex network of canals and pumps that keep the ever-encroaching swamps at bay.

Just outside the city limits there are several wonderful parks that allow for hiking and canoeing through the marshy wetlands. One of my favorite spots is a swamp where there are raised boardwalks that run alongside several bayous for a couple of miles. The wildlife and foliage of the swamp abound alongside this pathway which allows visitors to journey into the dark, nested depths of this natural beauty.

I learned from someone, much to the horror of park rangers no doubt, that alligators like marshmallows. That's right—white, fluffy marshmallows. All I had to do was toss one of those marshmallows out into the bayou, then sit back and wait. In a matter of minutes, a pair of eyes would surface and silently glide through the water toward the white, bobbing morsel of sugar. Almost magically, two eyes would become four and four eyes would become six, then eight. I would watch the bushes growing over the water's edge as, invariably, alligators would slink out of the shade and paddle over to the marshmallow. Soon, often without warning, one of the brave reptiles would lunge forward and steal the marshmallow with a quick, powerful snap.

What was mysterious (and really creepy) was the fact that these alligators had silently been watching me all along. No doubt, they and countless others had watched me hike for the mile or so through the swamp and along the bayou. Their piercing eyes and acute sense of smell had sensed the presence of flesh and blood and they had stalked me like any other prey. All the while, I was completely unaware of their hungry vigil. It wasn't until I tossed the marshmallow out into the water that they abandoned their hiding places in the brush and cypress trees that lined the bank and revealed their presence.

Those alligators are like our memories. Even when we think we are alone and totally free, powerful memories swim just beneath the murky waters of our awareness. Just behind the bushes that grow in the landscapes of our lives are many unsuspected eyes that watch us and, if we allow, control us.

> **More often than not, we are unaware of the memories which impinge on our perception of the present.**

What we like to eat, who we choose as friends and lovers, how we feel about what happens to us, and how we react to circumstances are all influenced by the memory of our past experiences.

Sometimes, our memories of the past hold us back from creating a better future. We become prisoners of what we have known. When we refuse to reexamine the past, we become slow to change and cling to the old, familiar ways that have served us well. In short, we stagnate.

The past always remains with us. We cannot voluntarily forget the past. There is no mental eraser that frees us from the events that live within our brains. We can, however, learn new ways to think about those past events. By combining our memories with new data, we can see past events in a new light. The memories stay the same, but our reaction to those memories changes as we learn and grow.

Memory is a very powerful force in our lives. For anyone wanting to harness this power, memory has two critical aspects:

1. Present and future behavior is heavily influenced by memories of the past.
2. Memories, while enduring, can be reinterpreted with new information.

THE PRESENT INFLUENCE OF THE PAST

We *give* memories extraordinary power over our lives. Yes, we give them their power. Past events cannot reach into the present and control us unless we allow them to do so. Like those alligators gliding through dark waters, they are harmless, unless we place ourselves in a vulnerable place where they can control us.

Consider the ancient Greek myth of Psyche and Eros:

Once upon a time, there was a beautiful young woman. In fact, she was the loveliest woman in the world. Although the other young ladies of her age married and started families, she did not. Her radiant beauty, it seemed, made her too perfect for any mere mortal. Her name was Psyche.

Psyche's parents, distressed over their beautiful daughter's predicament, consulted the great oracle at Delphi. The oracle's answer was even more distressing: Psyche must die. She must be dressed in funeral clothes and taken to the mountains on the far side of the kingdom. There she was to be left to die.

So the parents obeyed the great oracle and left Psyche in the cold and windy mountains. As she lay there, numb with fear, Eros, the god of passionate love, came to her rescue. When his eyes fell upon her perfect face, he fell desperately in love with her. With the help of his friend, the West Wind, he whisked her away to his hidden palace.

When she awoke, Psyche found herself in the most luxurious place she had ever been. She had everything she could possibly want; there was food, drink, lovely clothing, perfumed baths. When evening came and the darkness fell, Eros came to her and slept with her. Night after night he did this. Psyche could not have asked for more. She was deliriously happy.

In time, however, Psyche wished to see her lover. What did he look like? Perhaps he was a monster, so hideous that he could only appear under the veil of darkness? Her curiosity and suspicions about Eros grew and eventually filled her head. She vowed to find out the truth.

Late one night, after Eros had fallen asleep, she crept out and found a candle. She lit the candle in the hall, and tiptoed up to the bed where he slept. Lifting the candle over his bed, she cast her gaze upon her lover. There he slept, the handsomest of gods! She was so excited, she jerked the candle, causing a drop of wax to land on Eros. It awoke him, and realizing that Psyche had broken the rules, he disappeared.

Psyche then began a journey from the wonderful castle to find her lover. Her grief was so great, she gained the sympathy of Eros's mother, the great goddess Aphrodite. Aphrodite told Psyche that she was not strong enough to do what must be done to win back Eros. Psyche vowed that she would do anything.

"Very well," said Aphrodite. "You must complete the four tasks."

Aphrodite then explained each task in order. First, Psyche must sort out a roomful of seeds—putting each type of seed in a separate pile. This must be completed in a single night. Second, Psyche must go to the field where the golden fleece is guarded by fire-breathing rams and bring back some of the fleece. It was well known that the rams killed anyone who tried to get past them. Third, Psyche must fetch a goblet of water from the River Styx that flows through the heavens and into the underworld.

Finally, Psyche must descend into hell and ask Persephone for a box of a magic ointment that makes one eternally beautiful.

Psyche was overwhelmed. Grief-stricken at the impossibility of these tasks, she opened the door to the room of seeds. The seeds were piled far above her head. She bent over and began sorting the seeds. Big, little, brown, black, there were so many! The enormity of the task overcame her, and she wearily cried herself to sleep beside the pile of seeds.

In the morning, she awoke to find that a great army of ants had come to her rescue and sorted all of the seeds. She jumped for joy, and then began her second task. Just as she approached the field of fire-breathing rams, the reeds that grew beside the river whispered to her the secret to getting the golden fleece. She must wait until evening and when the rams were resting, creep in and steal a bit of coveted fleece. She did as the reeds said, and she got a handful of the golden fleece.

As in the previous two tasks, nature was on Psyche's side for the third task. A great eagle swooped down, taking the goblet from her hands and returned with it full of water from the river Styx.

Finally, she was faced with the fourth and most difficult task: descending to the underworld. Just as she was on the verge of giving up, a tower near her began speaking. The tower told her to bring coins to pay for her passage across the Styx and to carry cakes to pacify the animals which guard the underworld. She did as the tower instructed, and successfully retrieved the magic ointment.

Exhausted, but jubilant, she made her way back to Aphrodite. Along the way, she was tempted to open the box of ointment. Why should Aphrodite alone enjoy its wonderful contents? The temptation overwhelmed her and she opened the box. The magic of the potion was too strong for a mere mortal and Psyche collapsed under its power.

No sooner had she fallen than Eros came to her rescue, carrying her limp body to Mount Olympus where Psyche was made immortal.

This is the point of decision for Psyche. What power will she give to her memories? On the one hand, will she remember with horror the feeling of sudden abandonment when Eros suddenly vanished from her bed? Will she ever more question the commitment of their relationship? Or will she cherish the struggle that ultimately brought back to her the most important thing in her life? How will she feel about her mother-in-law, the great Aphrodite, who created the four tasks? Will she feel betrayed by Aphrodite who sent her on an impossible crusade? Or will she gain confidence from the fact that nature always provided a solution for her just when she needed it and allowed her to be reunited with Eros?

The myth of Psyche and Eros underscores the role of memory in controlling our lives. Regardless of the past event, what counts is our *interpretation* of that event. Will we frame that event in a way that allows us to thrive in the present? Or will we frame it in a way that slows and embitters us? We can assign our memories the power to help or hinder us. As it turns out, Psyche chose to frame her memories positively and the two of them lived happily ever after.

Likewise, employees are influenced by the way they choose to remember the past. For better or worse, employees carry with them reminiscences of each job they hold, each experience with a supervisor, and every new and discarded corporate objective; in short, everything that has happened to them at work. Each employee has an investment in the past, an investment that grows larger with each passing day. It is an investment that has great power over her current performance, depending on hows she interprets the past in relation to the present. Consider this real-life example.

CAMELOT, INC.

I once worked for a comfortable family business that had grown exponentially over the forty years prior to being sold to a national conglomerate. Despite the growth, this company had continued to be run as if it were a mom-and-pop operation. Hard-working people worked there and all employees were considered family.

After the sale, the new parent company announced sweeping changes. The new managers had little regard for the way things had always been done. As far as they were concerned, it was a new day and everyone better get with the program. To the employees, the new managers seemed to sneer at the old ways.

The employees of this company were quite competent and committed, but they had one thing the new management hadn't accounted for: they cherished how things used to be. They had an emotional investment in a past they had built with hard work and sweat. The past was fondly labeled "Camelot" and they remembered it with great affection.

The new managers tried to force change to no avail. The more they pushed, the more the organization seemed to flop down like a stubborn mule. The past— their past—had been insulted. It wasn't so much that the new ways were flawed, it was that by practicing them, the past seemed invalidated. Doing business the new way seemed to say that the old way was wrong, and that was something none of the old guard was willing to admit. Besides, the old ways had been successful for more than forty years, why change now? Ultimately, two CEOs and scores of vice presidents failed trying to force change on an organization that tenaciously clung to the past.

These managers could have accomplished great changes if they had only respected the power of the past.

If they had taken the time to learn about the past and to build upon it, they could have slowly introduced changes that would have complemented and refined the previous ways. Employees, on the other hand, would have had time to accommodate and accept the changes, instead of resisting.

Instead, the new managers tried to ignore the past. Impatient and ambitious, they tried to discard what happened yesterday and declared a new day, "out with the old and in with the new!' They admonished employees to forget the past. With new organization charts and job descriptions, they brought the company to its knees, reconfigured the players and then try to jump-start it to immediate full throttle.

As it was for that organization, discontinuous, radical change is most often disastrous. To begin with, the past has been invalidated and discarded. When the past is defamed in this way, every employee shares in the shame—an emotion that destroys personal power and creativity.

> **No amount of proclaiming a new day and a clean slate will change the memory of yesterday. If the fondly remembered past is blasphemed, it will rise again and strike back at its detractors.**

Only with gentle prodding and continuous help will employees change their interpretation of the past.

The power of memory is all-encompassing and no manager can afford to ignore it. Employees are changed by every job they perform; toughened by every conflict and disappointment, enlivened by each victory. Each success and failure burrows its way into their consciousness, guiding their present actions and shaping expectations for the future.

REFRAMING

To effectively use the power of memory for good, the manager must consistently help employees to understand and *transcend* the past; to use the past as a virtual ladder to lift them to higher plane than where they were before.

By building on the past, the manager can ride its momentum, gaining great leverage toward new objectives. He gently guides the forces of yesterday toward the goals of tomorrow. This kind of change is gradual and thoughtful, but in the end it is successful.

While we may not be able to erase past memories, we can learn to think about them differently. By combining our memories with new information, we can redirect the power of memory. The is the process of *reframing*.

Reframing takes what happened in the past and uses it to propel and support the present. Memories that once brought great pain, can be reinterpreted in the present to elicit far less traumatic emotions (this, in essence, is the work of every therapist). For example, the embarrassing and painful memory of repeating the first grade can be reinterpreted in adulthood as a positive experience. The realization that the "failure" probably spared one a future of comparative immaturity turns it into a positive. It is the same event, only reinterpreted in the light of new information.

Reframing is one of the great secrets of organizational change. Managers who successfully change an organization do so by carefully assessing what already exists and, where possible, they capitalize on and celebrate the assets of the past. This kind of respectful reorganization speaks volumes to even the most resistant of employees. It builds trust and enthusiasm for the change.

A BOMB GOES OFF

One of the most remarkable examples of a manager who worked the miracle of transcending the past comes from the bombing of the Murrah Federal Building in Oklahoma City. On April 19th of 1995, Florence Rogers, CEO of Federal Employees Credit Union (FECU), summoned seven of her top managers into her office. As she turned to face the group, a huge explosion ripped through the room. Rogers was thrown against a far wall. The floor of her third-story office collapsed. Everyone but Rogers plummeted to their deaths.

Perched on a precarious 18-inch ledge, Rogers hollered for help. Two rescue workers carried her to safety. Most of her staff weren't so lucky. All tolled, she lost 18 of her 32 employees in the most infamous terrorist act in recent American history.

Raymond Stroud, Comptroller at FECU was pulled out of a meeting he was attending in Tampa, Florida and told what had happened within minutes of the blast. He left the conference room and went to his hotel room where he switched on CNN. "When I saw those pictures of the federal building, I just knew no one could have survived," he remembers.

Stroud immediately called his travel agent and within two hours, was on a plane back to Oklahoma City. On the flight back, he occupied himself by reviewing lists of priorities from the credit union's disaster recovery plan and drawing maps of downtown for the many media reporters who were also on the plane. Unaware that Rogers had survived, he wasn't sure what he would find when he landed. Little did he know that he was the only surviving vice president.

In the 48 hours after that tragedy, both Rogers and Stroud faced the biggest challenges of their careers. Not only did they have to pick up the pieces of a shattered office, they had to be back in business for the credit union members, many of which had lost several family members and needed access to money immediately for medical and funeral expenses. What was more, they had to do it all with less than half a staff, all of whom were badly shaken and many who were physically injured.

The job was overwhelming. They had to move the offices, hire new employees, and recreate the transactions which were destroyed. In the weeks that followed, the surviving management worked 80-hour workweeks. Even though they had a thorough disaster recovery plan, it had one overwhelming flaw: the plan had assumed that most, if not all employees would be returning to work after the disaster. Who would have imagined a disaster that would not only eliminate the facilities, but many of the employees as well?

Much to the credit of Rogers and Stroud, the credit union's telephone system which allowed members to check on their accounts was up and running within 24 hours of the bombing. By 48 hours, teller services were restored and a new, temporary location for the credit union had been secured. Within a week, the credit union was fully staffed with surviving employees, replacement workers and volunteers from other credit unions. By year's end, almost all transactions which were destroyed in the bomb blast had been successful recreated.

The staff, however, was still reeling with the shock of it all. Tellers would suddenly burst into tears when they saw a name on a check or a customer that brought back memories of co-workers that were gone. Angry outbursts weren't uncommon and several of the surviving staff quit, unable to deal with the stress of it all.

Compounding the problem, some of the surviving employees were promoted into positions that had been opened by superiors who were killed. Not only was it difficult for them to accept these promotions, once given the position, they were hesitant to make any changes, feeling that change would disrespect the memory of the deceased employee.

Amy Petty, was promoted into her boss's job in the credit card department. Petty describes the torment she went through feeling that she couldn't benefit from the horrible blast that killed her boss, Vicki. It seemed like "blood money" to accept a raise in the shadow of Vicki's death. Further, she recalls how difficult it was to change any of the processes Vicki had put in place. To change the job, even if it was an improvement, felt like a dishonor to Vicki's memory.

The stress created by the tragedy put enormous strain on working relationships. Stroud describes it this way: "After the bomb good relationships got better, and stressed relationships got even more stressed. If you worked well with someone before the bomb, then your working relationship tended to get better. If there were conflicts before, they escalated afterwards."

Stroud describes two things that the credit union management did which helped employees to handle what had happened. First was a policy that allowed the surviving employees the freedom to take time to recover and deal with the emotions of the situation openly. Stroud says, "We told them to take time. If you're having a bad day, take some time off. Go home, no questions asked. Do what you need to do to feel better." Managers helped alleviate the pressure by identifying backup replacements who could take over the job of absent employees.

Stroud, a boy-next-door, late thirty-something manager doesn't come across as the "touchy-feely" type, yet he admits that he had his moments. "There were times when the tears came and I needed hugs, too." What helped him to transcend the difficult memories were the counselors which the Credit Union National Association provided to any employee of the credit union. According to Stroud, "Those counselors were one of the best things that ever happened to us, especially me."

Second, Stroud reframed the past by talking about a "*new* normal." He says, "members would come in and ask 'when are things going to get back to normal?' and I would reply 'we will never have the old normal again, we now have a new normal.'" The concept of a new normal began to take hold around the credit union. The past was gone. Friends and co-workers were lost. Now, the survivors were creating a *new* normal that didn't invalidate what was before.

The new normal was very real for the survivors. Stroud talks fondly about an accountant, Jill, who worked for him and was killed by the bomb. "She was just a really neat person," he remembers, but quickly says that his new accountant isn't less than Jill, she's just a different person. "And, at first, I had to remind myself of that often."

The new normal honored the past. In the year following the blast, there was no hesitancy to talk about the deceased employees by name. Despite the overwhelming temptation to ignore the painful memories, managers dealt with their feelings and the feelings of employees openly. Staff meetings in the weeks following the blast, started with a rundown on the status of missing employees and the schedule of funerals. Every day, more bodies were found and the list of those unaccounted for eventually dwindled.

Rogers, a thirty-five year veteran of the credit union and the person who had steered its growth from a meager $1 million institution had personally hired most everyone who worked there. Her influence was so much a part of the credit union, employees affectionately labeled her "the Old Lead Goose." Rogers did many things to both honor the past and, at the same time, create the new normal. Among the most moving is this memo she wrote and shared with the surviving employees and members. Here is an excerpt:

"Memo to my dear lovely ladies from the Old Lead Goose:

I truly don't understand why so many of you had to be taken out of our formation at one time. It's going to be difficult in the days and weeks ahead to keep our meager remaining flock on course as we fly on to our destination. Some of our flock was wounded and will not be able to join our migration for awhile. New little ones will take up your places so we can continue on. The ones that take flight with us will be carefully picked to ensure a safe, successful journey and make you proud so that your legacy will live on.

Today, I can just visualize all you beautiful gals now in your new location in heaven. Your dedication and enthusiasm has gone with you and you're probably starting up the "heavenly credit union" where the field of membership is open to all. . .

Sonja, you will prepare the training sessions so everyone will know their roles and places in line. . .

Frankie, Christy and Tresia, keep smiling as you did here on earth, instilling confidence and giving of yourself with that personal touch which made everyone feel so special. . .

Kathy, Leinen and Claudine, the only collecting you will now need to do is new friends and the only counseling will be with the new arrivals. . .

Vicki, you will no longer worry about credit cards, but instead you can issue passes to the streets that are paved with gold. . .

You all would be so proud to know how many loved you and how many of your credit union friends came to our rescue to ensure our safe recovery. . .they flew in from everywhere to assist and gave untiring efforts and did so much in your honor. You'd be so proud. . .

I know you are urgently seeking a way to send your loved ones here on earth an e-mail from your new location. I will volunteer to tell them today what it will say if that's okay with you. . . .do not stand at my grave and weep. . .

You will be missed so much, but just remember, the old flock will all be together one day and our worries will be few when we reach our final destination.

Sincerely,
The Old Lead Goose left on earth to continue the flight,
Florence Rogers

With this memo, Rogers sent a heartfelt message filled with her own beliefs about heaven. It wasn't a glossing over, but an honest statement of her sorrow and, more important, her focus on the future. She opened her heart to the employees and let them know why she was able to move forward, and how that could honor the memory of those who were past. The employees didn't have to accept her belief in heaven; the memo helped them understand how *she* was dealing with the past and why she could move on without treading upon the memory of those who were lost. In her own way, she honored their humanity.

With constant messages about honoring the past by moving forward, the credit union slowly emerged from the tragedy. Stroud remembers, "At first, all of the grief interfered with work, but as time went on, the names of those killed were spoken less and less. In time, we were able to put it all aside, at least, long enough to get our work done."

And they did more than get the work done. Two years after the bombing, despite the initial threat of either closing the doors or being absorbed by another credit union, the assets have grown by more than $8 million to a total of $80 million. Member confidence in viability of the credit union has never been higher, and a new building which will triple the current square footage is under construction. A second location was opened recently to handle new business and as a convenience to downtown customers.

The story of this credit union is a dramatic story of what can happen when managers use rather than fight the memory of employees. By working with the momentum of the past, managers can control it and change its direction. Damming that momentum through denial and repression requires enormous energy and builds a counterforce for change.

Even though this story is more extreme than the situations most managers are likely to face, it is the extremity that highlights some very important points. In this example, the ultimate futility of the usual "stiff upper lip" approach managers take toward the past comes across loud and clear. All too often, managers try to erase the power of the past by ignoring it. Had this happened at the Federal Employees' Credit Union in Oklahoma City, there is no question in the minds of its management or employees that the credit union would have failed to recover, much less grow and prosper.

While most managers aren't dealing with the death of employees, they are regularly dealing with mass layoffs, reorganizations and strategy shifts. All of these create a sense of loss based on a past that exists no more. There is much to be learned from examples like that of the Oklahoma City Federal Employees' Credit Union about transcending a painful past and moving forward to a more successful future.

THE POWER OF BUILDING POSITIVE MEMORIES

Rather than spending energy reframing the past, some very wise managers have built extraordinary memories from the start. One such manager was David Packard.

Never before, and not since, have I known a company whose employees were so fiercely loyal and protective of the business. Hewlett-Packard employees are proud to be part of an organization that they consider to be a notch or two above the rest. On any given workday, the parking lots of HP facilities fill up at 7:00 A.M. and don't empty until almost 7:00 P.M. The employees work hard and, for the most part, gladly do whatever is required to make the company succeed, making HP one of the most continually successful companies in Silicon Valley.

How does a company like this form? David Packard did it, in large part, creating positive memories from the start. Packard understood that every action his managers took lived on in the memories of employees. He established a strong system of values which he published and labeled the HP Way. All management decisions were required to conform to these values which included, among other things, an open-door management policy, treating employees with respect, and paying employees among the market leaders.

Stories of how Packard clung to these values abound within the organization. One story tells how, when a new facility was built that had corner offices with carpet and doors, Packard arrived at the scene and demanded that they be torn out. His managers were to be shoulder to shoulder with employees, not hiding behind a closed door or in a reclusive executive office. Clearly more of a symbolic gesture than a cost-conserving measure, that happened in the mid-1960s and yet the story lives on, embedded in the memories of employees.

Another memory of long-term employees includes the time that Packard discovered one his employees had been financially devastated by a long-term illness. He called all of the employees together on the main corporate campus and declared that this would never happen to an HP employee again, announcing the beginning of HP's comprehensive medical coverage of all employees. This memory dates back to the early 1950s and the story is still told today.

One of the secretaries at HP tells the story of when she used to work on one of HP's many manufacturing lines. She remembers the day that Packard showed up, unannounced, on the loading dock where the line workers normally ate their bag lunches. He, too, produced a bag lunch and spent the hour talking with the workers about their job experiences and suggestions for improvement. She was clearly impressed that the president of an international company was interested in her ideas.

These kinds of memories are incredibly powerful. They continue to affect workers long after the actual event has passed. They inspire continued loyalty and commitment to the company and, more importantly, to its success.

Conversely, memories of managers engaging in cut-throat practices or dumping employees at the first sign of financial difficulty also live in the memory of employees. These memories continually remind employees that there is no reciprocal commitment between themselves and the company. The negative effect on morale and loyalty continues to affect employee behavior, long after the event has occurred.

Simply redrawing an organization on a piece of paper doesn't create a new organization. The force of memory always remains. The manager who uses that force can work miracles of change. Those who don't, may find themselves stuck in the mire of resistance.

CREATING THE MIRACLE

Here are a few suggestions for creating the miracle of transcending the past:

◆ *Celebrate endings.* When an employee leaves the company, throw a going away reception. When yearly goals are met, take the staff to lunch. When the department is reorganized, recognize and honor the work produced in the previous jobs. By marking and honoring the past with celebrations, you help to connect the past with the present and the future you would like to create. They help your "surviving" staff to make the transition.

◆   *Talk about the past, even when it may be difficult.* If an employee is fired, don't try to wipe their name and memory from the department. When appropriate, recall their good work. If employees are laid off, don't try to sweep it under the rug. Set a time and place to discuss what has happened. When an employee is experiencing a divorce, find an appropriate time to express your support and sympathy. By acknowledging the past, you are communicating your interest and care for employees. Whether they show it or not, they have an investment in the past, and when you honor that investment, you honor them.

◆   *Don't suddenly become critical of the previous strategy when there is a major shift in organizational strategy.* Instead, focus on the benefits of the past and how the new strategy will capitalize upon and expand them. Draw a mental line from the past strategy to the present, giving employees a context to understand and accept the changes. By suddenly denouncing yesterday's management decisions, you (who were part of those decisions) look insincere. Did you not mean what you said just yesterday when you were supporting the old strategy? Or are you now just mouthing the new management propaganda? Such criticism is confusing and frustrating to employees.

Affirmations

I acknowledge the past. I will not ignore it, but use it to honor the present.

I will accept the past as one link in a long chain which extends into the present and the future.

I will celebrate the victories of the past. I will honor those who won them. I will find the path that leads from past victories to present, greater victories.

On Becoming

*True abundance can only come
from internal abundance*

SUCCESS COMES FROM WITHIN.

It is true that profit can be made through dishonesty. Status can be acquired without integrity. Large organizations can be built without trust. Successful careers can be passionless. But true abundance—the experience of sufficiency and fulfillment—can occur only when it grows from abundance that begins inside a person. Money, success, power, status, property, and fame are empty unless they first emerge from an integrated self, one where actions, values and feelings are consistent and closely intertwined. The integrated self is the source of lasting satisfaction.

Nevertheless, we often work as if external abundance will make us happy and fulfilled. If only we could make more money, climb one more rung on the corporate ladder, win a bigger budget, hire a few more employees, sell another million widgets—we tell ourselves that this will give us the internal abundance we crave. Whatever it takes. Whatever the cost. We sell ourselves, and with it our happiness, while doggedly trying to earn happiness. It is a vicious treadmill with no end.

No amount of money, power or status will make us fulfilled if we can't live with ourselves after we have acquired these things. When we cunningly manipulate others, break our promises or intentionally deceive others for personal gain, we lose trust in humanity. We can no longer trust anyone else, for we know we can't trust ourselves. Despite the conquest, we are forced to enjoy our bounty with one eye constantly tuned for attack.

When we treat our relationships as commercial transactions, when we adopt convenient facades to manipulate others, we do so at great personal cost: our ability to have fulfilling relationships. We can no longer trust the apparent feelings of others, for they must be trying to get something from us. Slowly we close ourselves to a world that we have projected from our own deceptions. We no longer believe in unconditional love, we can no longer trust appearances however sincere they may appear. So we surround ourselves with beautiful possessions—the people we have manipulated and deceived—all the time knowing that if they knew who we really were, they would abandon us. This is the disintegrated self; it is a self where feelings and values have been traded for the possessions of success.

> *Better keep yourself clean and bright; you are the*
> *window through which you must see the world.*
>
> GEORGE BERNARD SHAW [35]

True abundance comes only from the path that strives for integration, where values are treasured and honored. This is *integrity*. Without it, success fails to satisfy. With integrity, we find a deeper satisfaction and contentment in our lives. This is the prize we sought when we started our journey in business. It is the path of the seven miracles.

The other path, the way of dis-integrity is largely responsible for the sense of alienation that has proliferated throughout society in the late twentieth century. What is real? What is true? What is sincere? We can't trust ourselves. We don't know what we believe. We are disassociated from our true self.

Our world reflects our own dis-integrity. We shop in malls lined with facades that are designed to manipulate our feelings. We eat in "theme" restaurants which are pale imitations of other cultures. We watch actors on television whose handsome faces and chiseled bodies create an unattainable ideal. Nevertheless, we try to change our bodies in gyms lined with mirrors and our faces with cremes, acids and surgery. All this in an effort to be something else, something which we have decided is far better than what nature has given.

IMPOSTORS

Over the past fifty years, psychologists have documented this sense of alienation in various forms. Dr. Pauline Clance measured what she called "the impostor phenomenon," a feeling that one doesn't deserve the successes they have achieved.[36] It is the feeling that one is concealing secrets about oneself accompanied by the fear that one day this "ugly" truth will be revealed.

Everyone has experienced at one point in life the feeling of being "out of place," but increasingly, particularly in business, more are reporting an overwhelming feeling of being an impostor. They privately report feeling their abilities are not sufficient for their level of achievement. Coupled with this insecurity, mid-career executives often do not know "what they want to be when they grow up." Nothing seems to hold much allure or enchantment. It all seems to be little more than a very harried, exasperating game. Nothing they have done in their career or that they might attempt in the future seems to achieve any real significance.

This malaise has spread throughout the modern organization. Morale continues to wane, and we blame everyone but ourselves for the problem. We fault management, long working hours, stress, competitors, and so forth. While all of these have a legitimate role to play in demeaning the work environment, they are not the real problem. The problem lies within ourselves and our own lack of an integrated self. Rather than discover values which are meaningful and life-directing, we are adrift in the sea of our own life, without direction or purpose. What employer could satisfy us when, in reality, we don't know who we are or what we want from our lives?

The path to true abundance requires us to take a hard look at ourselves. It means stripping away the layers of sheepskins we have piled upon ourselves, to discover who we are, and what is meaningful in our lives. We must cling to this discovery and pursue it at all costs. Only once we have given it everything, do we find the treasure of our lives.

If you will take the seven miracles and apply them to your life and work, you can not help but find yourself. The harder you work at finding the right idea to manifest, the more you will discover what is truly worthwhile. As you begin to treat others as you would like to be treated, you come to know what you want in your relationships. When you commit to honesty, no matter what the cost, you shed the masks behind which you have been hiding and discover what is truth. Down the line, each of the seven miracles will not only change your organization, it will change your life for the better.

EQUAL TIME

Dr. Ruth Elmer, a respected New Orleans minister for the past forty years, has a wonderful method for beginning this journey of integrity. She tells her congregation that the best way to change for the better is to give "equal time" to the new way. Instead of trying to do an about-face, require yourself to engage in the new behaviors at least as often as you fall into the old behavioral patterns. No condemnation or guilt, simply attempt to give your new values equal time.

No one can begin to practice all seven miracles perfectly. Every day you may find yourself reverting to old behaviors, ignoring the values you have hoped to practice. Instead of chiding yourself for the mistake, simply give the new behaviors equal time. When you have fallen into the old patterns of dishonesty, intentionally take other actions that are sincere and honest. As you do, you will discover the new behaviors slowly replacing the older, less desirable ones. Without self-flagellation, you will discover positive change overwhelming your life.

The seven miracles are about a career of becoming your personal best. You will never arrive at your destination, but you will find great fulfillment in the journey itself. The journey is not linear, but rather a curvilinear spiral that moves forward by constantly circling backwards. Lessons learned, victories savored, and storms weathered come back to us again and again, each time teaching us more about ourselves. The key lies not in trying to control the circumstances, but in changing ourselves with learning.

Volumes have been written about "managing change" in the past decade and much of this has focused on controlling the circumstances of organizational change. While there is no harm in softening the blow of change, the real solution lies within ourselves. When we have found our treasure within, no circumstance, no reorganization, no job change, can threaten us for we know that our happiness depends upon how we handle the situation and not in what the organization does to us.

That doesn't excuse abusive corporate practices. It is simply that the answer to many of the problems facing the modern corporation lie within ourselves and not with the usual targets of blame.

The fact is, the more in tune we are with ourselves, the more difficult it becomes for us to behave in ways that hurt other people. As we know ourselves and experience our own pains and joys, we also become more empathetic to the experience of others. For example, when we allow ourselves to be vulnerable and trust employees, we are far less likely to take advantage of someone else who is experiencing the same vulnerability. It is only the manager who has separated himself from his own feelings who can callously deceive and exploit others.

It is through internal abundance that we heal the corporate community. By healing ourselves, we heal the larger organization of which we are a member. There is no other path to corporate healing.

THE CORPORATE COMMUNITY

The corporation is a community where all the parts are connected to each other. When one part interacts with another, every part is affected. When one part changes, every part must move to accommodate that change.

The interrelatedness of community is poignantly illustrated by a modern "parable" that has appeared in books and speeches, particularly in the area of ecology, over the past twenty years. Although no one seems to know the source of this story, it is quite plausible and worth repeating for metaphorical purposes.[37]

It seems that the World Health Organization attempted to eliminate malaria-carrying mosquitoes in the remote villages of Borneo with DDT. The aerial spraying of the pesticide was quite successful in eliminating the mosquitoes and the disease they carried. However, shortly thereafter the number of cases of plague began to rise dramatically. Also, rather curiously, the thatched roofs of the village longhouses began to collapse.

Upon investigation it was discovered that lizards eventually accumulated DDT in their bodies and died. This, in turn, killed the village cats which ate the lizards. As a result, the village rat population exploded and with the rats came the unhealthful fleas which cause plague. And the thatched roofs that were collapsing? This happened because the insects which live in the thatched roofs were immune to DDT and multiplied due to the decreased lizard population.

Prior to the well-intentioned intervention the villagers, insects, lizards, and cats had lived in a balanced community, each interdependent upon the other. The spraying of DDT, which was intended to affect only one part of that living system, changed the entire community.

This story illustrates the truth of our interconnectedness. Even when we think our actions will affect only a small part of the organization, those actions potentially affect the entire organization. We are all connected. How we manage ourselves and our employees affects the entire organization.

Unfortunately, many corporate managers strongly identify with the "rugged individualist" view of the corporation where "each man is for himself" and the corporation is little more than a loose federation of bandits. This view is an illusion. When we act upon others, we create a chain reaction that inevitably acts upon ourselves. What we do in the corporation not only affects every other employee, but ourselves in the end. In effect, we determine how the corporation treats us.

It is true that those with the greatest power can often create the greatest impact on the organization, but that doesn't negate the effect of the less powerful. The ripples created by the smallest pebbles can travel as far as those of the largest stone. While they may not be as powerful, they have nevertheless started the chain of reaction that spreads across the organization.

In quantum physics there is the idea of the "butterfly effect" which is based on the fact that nonlinear or chaotic systems are profoundly influenced by the conditions that initiate them. In essence, the smallest change can have a very large effect. The name "butterfly effect" comes from a metaphorical example that something as tiny and inconsequential as the flutter of a butterfly's wings can set up a chain of events, such as a growing interaction of atmospheric disturbances that eventually could result in a hurricane many thousands of miles away.

So it is in organizations. Sometimes the smallest event can set in motion dramatic consequences. When even the lowest level employee begins to practice the seven miracles, it can have dramatic effects throughout the organization.

Ground zero for positive organizational change is inside you and me. As we come to know the fullness of our being, acknowledging and honoring our humanity, we also change our attitudes and behavior toward others. As managers, when we change, we treat our employees differently, changing their environment and ultimately changing them. This is lasting organizational change. This is miraculous power. It is your power.

Notes

1. Nikhil Deogun, "Pepsi's Mr. Nice Guy vows not to finish last," *The Wall Street Journal*, March 19, 1997, p. B1.

2. Victor Frankl, *Man's Search for Meaning: An Introduction to Logotherapy*, (Boston: Beacon Press, 1959).

3. Daniel Goleman, *Emotional Intelligence: Why it can matter more than I*, (New York: Bantam Books, 1995).

4. George Santayana, *Dialogues in Limbo*, (London: Constable and Co. Ltd., 1925).

5. William James, *The Varieties of Religious Experience*, Lecture 20, 1902.

6. Beatrice Garcia, "Chainsaw Al is a stand-up kinda guy," *Miami Herald (Business Monday Supplement)*, September 15, 1997, p. 5.

7. David Bollier, *Aiming Higher*, (New York: AMA-COM, 1996).

8. James Allen, *As a Man Thinketh*, (Marina Del Ray, Calif.: DeVorss Publications, 1989).

9. Ralph Waldo Emerson, *The Conduct of Life*, 1860.

10. Proverbs 23:7.

11. Louis E. Boone, *Quotable Business*, (New York: Random House, 1992), p. 282.

12. Ron Schultz, *Unconventional Wisdom*, (New York: Harper Business, 1994), p. 5.

13. Robert Browning, *A Death in the Desert*. (New York: Ecco Press, 1990).

14. Ron Schultz, *Unconventional Wisdom*, (New York, Harper Business, 1994), p. 15.

15. Ron Schultz, *Unconventional Wisdom*, (New York: Harper Business, 1994), p. 16.

16. Margaret J. Wheatley, *Leadership and the New Science*, (San Francisco: Berrett Koehler, 1992).

17. Peter Burrows, "HP pictures the future," *Business Week*, July 7, 1997, p. 100.

18. Ellen Hale, "Selling or selling out? How community hospitals are changing hands," *Gannett News Service*, October 13, 1996, S11.

19. John Greenwald, *Time*, August 4, 1997, p. 46.

20. Ralph Waldo Emerson, *Essays*, Boston: 1876.

21. Maggie Jackson, "Nearly half of workers take unethical actions, cite pressures," *Associated Press*, April 5, 1997.

22. William C. Jennings, "A corporate conscience must start at the top," *The New York Times*,. December 29, 1996, p. 14.

23. Amar Bhide and Howard Stevenson, "Why be honest if honesty doesn't pay?" *Harvard Business Review*, September-October, 1990.

24. Alan Downs, *Beyond the Looking Glass: Overcoming the Seductive Culture of Corporate Narcissism*, (New York: AMACOM, 1997).

25. Mark Twain, *Autobiography*, New York: Harper & Bros., 1924), ch. 29.

26. Joe Morganstern, "The Fifty-Nine-Story Crisis," *The New Yorker*, May 29, 1995, p. 45-53.

27. Conrad Hilton, *Be My Guest*, (New York: Prentice Hall Press, 1957).

28. Elisabeth Kübler-Ross, *The Wheel of Life*, (New York: Scribner, 1997), p. 18.

29. Clare Ansberry, "Forgive and forget: Firms face decision," *The Wall Street Journal*, November 24, 1987.

30. Judith Martin, "Miss Manners," *The Washington Post*, August 3, 1997, p. F02.

31. Marjorie Kelly, "Why 'socially responsible' isn't enough," *Business Ethics*, July/August, 1997.

32. Frederick Herzberg, "One more time: How do you motivate employees?" *Harvard Business Review*, January-February, 1968. Reprinted with update, September-October, 1987.

33. Michael Powell, "Betrayal," *Inc.*, April 1996, p. 23.

34. Will Rogers, *The Autobiography of Will Rogers*, Boston: Houghton Mifflin Co., 1949).

35. George Bernard Shaw, *Man and Superman*, 1903.

36. Pauline Rose Clance, "The impostor phenomenon scale," *Psychotherapy: Theory, Research and Practice*, 1978, p. 241.

37. David Spangler, *Everyday Miracles: The inner art of manifestation*, (New York: Bantam, 1996), p. 50.

Index